Cane & Rush
Seating

CHARLOTTE LAHALLE

Published by Schiffer Publishing, Ltd.
4880 Lower Valley Road
Atglen, PA 19310
Phone: (610) 593-1777; Fax: (610) 593-2002
E-mail: Info@schifferbooks.com

For our complete selection of fine books on this and related subjects, please visit our website at www.schifferbooks.com. You may also write for a free catalog.

This book may be purchased from the publisher. Please try your bookstore first.

We are always looking for people to write books on new and related subjects. If you have an idea for a book, please contact us at proposals@schifferbooks.com.

Schiffer Publishing's titles are available at special discounts for bulk purchases for sales promotions or premiums. Special editions, including personalized covers, corporate imprints, and excerpts can be created in large quantities for special needs. For more information, contact the publisher.

Library of Congress Control Number: 2013948617

Type set in Flama/Arial

ISBN: 978-0-7643-4547-0
Printed in China

Cane & Rush
Seating

CHARLOTTE LAHALLE

4880 Lower Valley Road • Atglen, PA 19310

Table of Contents

Introduction

Caning and rush weaving are two distinct crafts, both in terms of the materials needed and the processes employed. What do they have in common? A skill for building and renovating seats.

Caning

Caning appeared in Europe as adventurers and merchants on the the the route to India brought back raw materials, including rattan, and the necessary skills to use them. In the East, rattan had been used for centuries to line seats and bedframes, using more or less sophisticated methods depending on the social class for which they were intended. Here, the chair-makers in the royal courts started using it to make their furniture lighter.

Arriving from England and the Netherlands, caning came into fashion in France in the 17th century, but it did not really take hold until the 18th century. Caned chairs were very popular under the Regency and Louis XV. They fulfil-led a desire for comfort and fantasy, and lent themselves perfectly to women's dresses with panniers, which held an increasingly impor-tant place in the salons.

This fashion continued during the reign of Louis XVI, with innovations such as golden and ceruse cane. It disappeared during the Revolution and the Empire, but made a come-back under Louis-Philippe and Napoleon III, albeit in a more austere form.

Until then, caning was done "hole-to-hole" (the cane strands passing alternatively above and below the wood, as explained in this book). In the 19th century, the invention of blind caning (where can strands are fixed into blind holes) made caning easier and opened it up to creativity, especially on chair backs.

In the early 20th century, Art Nouveau naturally integrated caning into its graphic concepts: purity, fluidity and repetition of intersecting lines. Meanwhile, the budding industry was dreaming up mechanical processes to reduce labor. Woven cane started to be sold by the meter. It was stretched over the seat, then bloc-ked under the seat with a large strand of rattan. Then all you had to do was cover it by hand to perfect the illusion. This method is still used today for mass produced caned furniture. Although convenient and quick, this method does away with the tiny imperfections that give hand caned items their charm.

If caning was long the domain of the nobility and the upper-middle classes, in 1860 it star-ted to move into cafés and public areas with Thonet's famous "bistro chair." At the same time, colonial inspiration gave birth to all sorts of exotic caned furniture in varying levels of intricacy.

Today, when styles are freely combined and juxtaposed, caning has a place in every home. Now, as then, we appreciate its lightness and technical simplicity, which lends itself to the most restrained and most fantastic shapes.

Straw Weaving

Straw used to be ubiquitous in the daily lives of people living in the countryside. Obviously it was used as animal fodder, but it was also used as fuel and for straw mattresses. It is difficult to pinpoint exactly when we got the idea to weave it onto seats. In France, it would seem that this technique was developed in the 14th century, in Provence – a region where this tradition is still alive today.

For a long time, straw weaving was a domestic activity practiced by peasants during the off-season, as were basket weaving and wicker fencing; raw materials abounded around the farms, and the strength of the structure was considered more important than its sophistication.

Still, craftsmen specialized in straw weaving, but they were mostly traveling artisans with low social status. They did not organize as a guild before they became liable to taxation in the 18th century. At the end of the 17th century, some of these craftsmen led entire villages to devote themselves primarily to the fabrication of straw-bottomed chairs: Iwuy in the North, Came in Basque Country, Neuville-Coppegueule in Somme, Cuisery and Rancy in Burgundy, etc. Although the chair caning industry has declined dramatically in the last century with the advent of mass production of furniture, some discerning workshops can still be found there.

Despite a brief craze at court under the Regency, thanks to one of those princely whims that launched trends, straw weaving has always occupied a modest place among French furniture. In middle class homes, it was confined to high chairs, children's chairs, and kitchen furniture. This could be due to its agricultural roots, or maybe to its technique, which only lends itself to simple shapes, keeping it from being adapted to many styles. Churches, however, remained faithful for a long time, with straw being a part of some Christian symbols (the straw of Jesus' manger, wheat straw for bread, etc.).

Simplicity is no longer scorned, but is rather a guarantee of authenticity and durability: straw weaving has finally acquired its pedigree. In all styles of homes, straw-work blends in harmoniously with all types of material: traditional or modern, simple or sophisticated. We love it for its simplicity and warmth, even more now that manufacturers make it in a wide range of delightful colors and textures.

Vocabulary of a seat

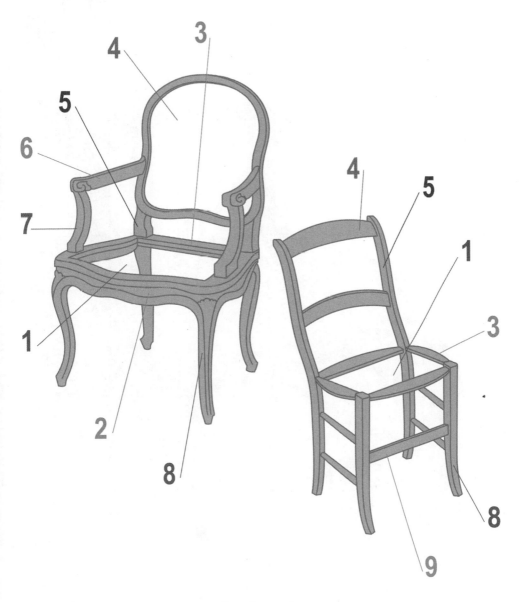

1	Seat	**6**	Armrest
2	Apron	**7**	Armrest upright
3	Crosspiece	**8**	Leg
4	Back	**9**	Stretcher
5	Back upright		

Caning

Although today there are faster methods using four or five cane strands, here you will find an explanation of the traditional six-strand technique, which results in a more solid and neat final product. There are four steps: laying the vertical cane strands, laying the horizontal cane strands, laying the diagonal cane strands, and binding. This guide is for working with seats; once mastered, it can easily be applied to chair backs and adapted for different shapes.

Materials

We only use cane—rattan bark mechanically cut into strong and evenly sized strands.

Cane is sold in hanks or coils of 250 g or 500 g. Cane strands measure from 1.5 m to 4 m, with a thickness of about 0.5 mm The widths available range from 2 mm to 4 mm.

For chair caning, it is important to buy top quality cane. Lower quality materials should only be used for decorative items.

Cane strand width

If the chair still has its old caning, measure the cane strand width. Otherwise, to figure out what width of cane to use, measure the the distance between the holes in the rim, which may be spaced differently from chair to chair (measure from the center of one hole to the center of the next), then use the table to the right.

You usually end up using three cane widths for one chair. For example, for a chair whose holes are 12 or 13 mm apart (the most common case), you should purchase:

- 2 mm-wide cane for laying the horizontal and vertical cane strands;
- 2.4 mm-wide cane for laying the diagonal cane strands;
- 3.5 mm-wide cane for laying the diagonal cane strands for binding (cane placed around the edge to hide the holes).

FYI

Older chairs don't have the final binding, so it's not necessary to get binder cane if you want to restore it to exactly what it looked like originally.

It may seem like a waste to buy an entire hank of cane for covering when all you need is one strand, but it has to have the specific width to properly cover the holes, regardless of their spacing.

On the other hand, it is possible to use one single cane width for the vertical, horizontal, and diagonal strands. If you are going to do that, choose an intermediate size (2.2 mm in the example below). Just be aware that the result will be less sophisticated.

Hole spacing	vertical or horizontal cane strands	diagonal cane strands
Less than 10mm	1.8mm	2.2mm
More than 10mm	2.2mm	2.6mm

Quantity

You will need 100 to 120 grams of cane to complete a chair with a standard frame. The length of cane strands within a hank or ring will vary. Use them all in full, without cutting them.

Preparing the cane

Unwind the cane or ring without unraveling the twine holding the cane strands together, so they don't get tangled. Pull out a strand, taking care not to damage it. The cane is fragile when dry. Handle it carefully and don't step on it, because that could split the cane strands, rendering them useless.

You should always wet the cane to soften it. Before putting a cane strand in the water, make sure it is in good condition. Get rid of any cane that is split or even slightly damaged; a tiny break can spread all along the cane strand.

Immerse the cane strand in a large container or a bathtub filled with cold water. Let it soak for five to ten minutes — it won't get softer if you let it soak longer than that. Take it out and wrap it in a towel to drain it.

You can soak three or four cane strands at a time and leave them in the towel until you are ready to use them. If the towel is damp, they won't have time to dry. However, it is preferable to soak the cane strands as you need them, since you should not get the cane wet more than once.

MAINTAINING CANE

Slack cane
Using a flat brush, apply a warm baking soda solution (one tablespoon of baking soda in a bowl of water) to both sides of the cane. Wipe with a cloth and let dry in a well-ventilated room.

Sagging cane
Wet the bottom of the cane liberally with a sponge soaked in boiling water. Let it dry in the sun.

Tools

A chair caner's tools are limited. You will find them at special caning and rush weaving stores, and in some craft stores.

AWL (1)
Consisting of a metal spike fixed into a wooden handle, the awl is useful for many tasks.

CANING COMB (2)
This is used to tighten the cane strands against each other. Commercially, you can now only find plastic combs. They are sold in sets of several models with different teeth spacing.

1 PAIR OF FLAT NEEDLES (3)
Although they are not essential, flat needles greatly facilitate laying the horizontal strands. They come in three lengths: 55 cm, 80 cm and 120 cm. They must be at least as long as the width of the seat.

WIRE CANING TOOL (4)
This tool consists of a wooden handle and a metal rod bent into an inverted V-shape. Some caners use it for laying the diagonal strands, but it is not essential.

DOWELS (5)
They are used to fix the cane strands into the holes in the frame. You will need four to cane a seat. Traditionally made of wood, dowels now come in brass. Their conical shape makes them work for all hole diameters.

You should also have:
• a cutter
• a small block of paraffin
• a large tub for soaking the cane
• a small sponge
• a rag

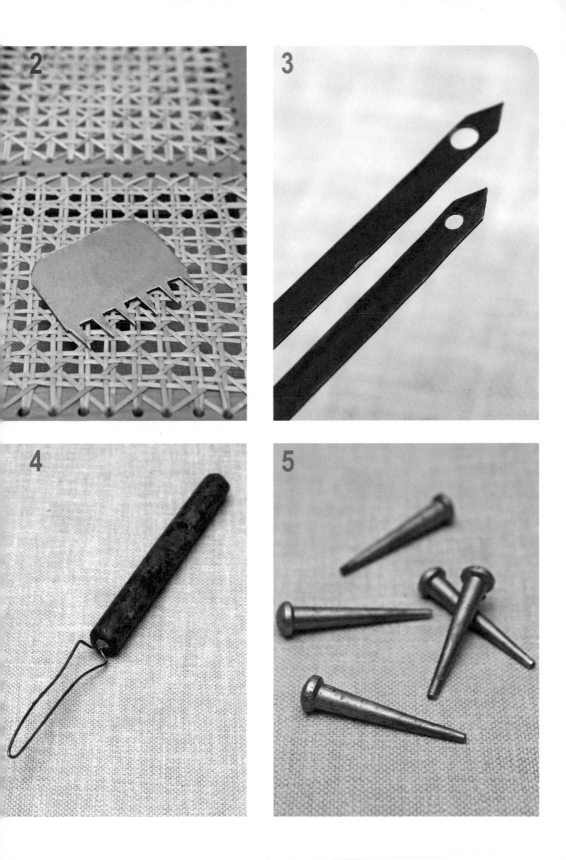

Preparing the seat

The chair structure sometimes makes it necessary to dismantle the seat frame. Basically, you need the holes to be accessible for threading cane strands through them.

Turn the chair over and see if the holes all around the frame are visible. If they are, you do not need to dismantle the chair. If they are not, remove the frame from the uprights by unscrewing the screws or, if it is simply fitted in, by hitting it a couple of times with a mallet, being careful not to damage the wood.

Start removing the old caning by cutting it around the edge with the cutter **(1)**.

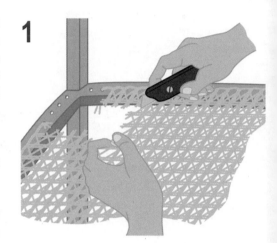

1

On the other side, remove all cane or wood residue by pulling them out one by one from each hole using an awl. The holes should be completely clear. On the "right" side of the frame, count the holes on the rear crosspiece to locate the middle one. Push in a dowel. Repeat this process on the front crosspiece **(2)**.

2

EVEN NUMBER OF HOLES IN FRONT AND BACK
Place the dowels in the first hole to left of the center of the crosspiece (3).

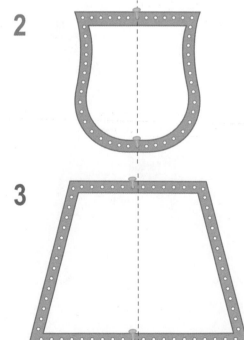

ODD NUMBER OF HOLES ON ONE CROSS-PIECE, EVEN NUMBER ON THE OTHERS
On the crosspiece where the number of holes is even, choose the one closest to the center.

3

ROUND SEAT
Take the location of the legs into account when determining the front and rear of the frame. There must be the same number of holes on either side of the dowels.

Vertical weaving

This first step involves stretching the vertical cane strands across the frame, over its entire width. You will lay two sets of strands in opposite directions to double each strand.

Right side

Starting hole

If the seat is round, start in the center of the frame, where you placed the dowels during preparation.

Otherwise, start on the third hole of the left rear corner (this will let you directly lay the horizontal strands with the current strand). Count the holes from the dowel placed in the center of the rear crosspiece to the third hole before the left corner; push in a dowel. On the front crosspiece, count the same number of holes in the same direction starting from the middle and push in a dowel **(1)**.

Laying the cane

Take a cane strand that is already wet. Thread it through the rear crosspiece starting hole, from below upwards, after removing the dowel **(2)**.

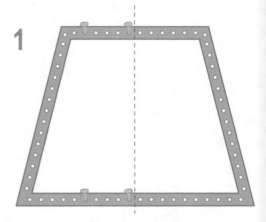

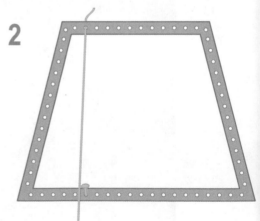

Remember

Throughout your work, be sure to place each strand right side up. The correct side of the strand is easily distinguished because it is slightly domed and glossier than the other side.

Pull the small end toward the inside of the frame. Insert it back into the starting hole, from bottom to top, making sure to overlap both ends in the hole **(3 and 4)**. When you tighten the working end, it will secure the tail end as long as it is pressed tight against the bottom. The tail should protrude 2 cm below the frame.

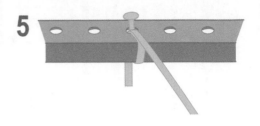

Tighten the working end by having it exactly overlap the loop so that the former covers the latter. Secure the whole thing with the dowel **(5)**.

Vertical Strands

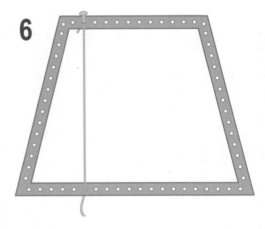

Thread the cane strand through the hole located opposite the front of the frame, from top to bottom, after removing the dowel **(6)**. Work with both hands: the top hand stretches the cane, and the bottom hand follows the movement **(7)**. Once it is tight enough, let go of the cane strand on top, hold it in position below, and quickly push a dowel into the hole to secure it.

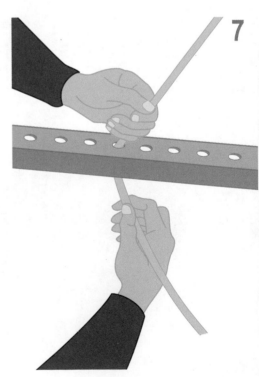

Make sure the cane strand is tight enough by plucking it like a harp cord - it should resonate. If it does not make any sound, it is not tight enough.

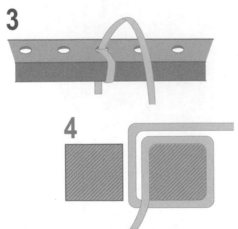

Pull the strand out through the next hole to the right **(8)**. Tighten it so that it is pressed against the wood under the frame. Make sure it is lying flat. If it is twisted, it may break very quickly. Push a dowel into this hole. Point the cane strand toward the rear crosspiece to thread it through the hole next to the starting hole **(9)**. Tighten it, then pull it out through the next hole. Keep working like this while maintaining a steady level of tension until you reach the right rear corner.

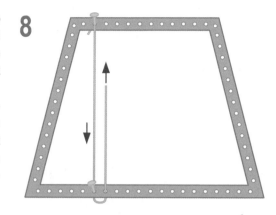

Rear Corner

ANGLED

At this point, the corner holes should be empty. If you thread the cane strand through them, it will go over some of the side holes, blocking them for the next strands **(10)**. Choose your holes on the lateral crosspiece so that all the vertical strands are parallel **(11)**.

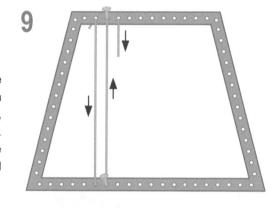

ROUNDED

Choose your holes on the lateral crosspiece so that all the vertical strands are parallel to the previous ones and regularly spaced. Sometimes you may have to skip holes to achieve this **(12)**.

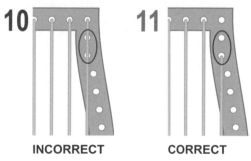

INCORRECT   **CORRECT**

FYI

Two dowels are enough for the project: one moves along the front crosspiece while the other moves along the rear crosspiece. Each time you thread the cane strand through a hole, it is essential to push in a dowel to maintain the tension.

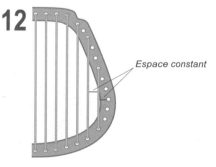

Espace constant

Joining Two Cane Strands

When one cane strand ends, join it to the next one with a knot as follows. Secure the first strand with a dowel and pull it out through the top of the next hole. Put the new cane strand in the same hole **(1)**.

On the other side, the old cane strand forms a link between the two holes. Thread the end of the new cane strand through the link, leaving a loop **(2)**. Pull the old cane strand on top to tighten the link and secure the new cane strand underneath. Make sure the new cane strand is right in the middle of the link, and not right next to a hole. Keep the old strand tight in one hand.

With the other hand, rethread the end of the new strand through the loop on the bottom of the crosspiece **(3)**, then pull the new strand on top.

When the strand is tight, let go of the old one: the knot is secure **(4)**. Make sure the strand is positioned correctly, then secure it by pushing a dowel into the hole. Cut the old strand 2 cm from the hole (it will be recut when you are finished).

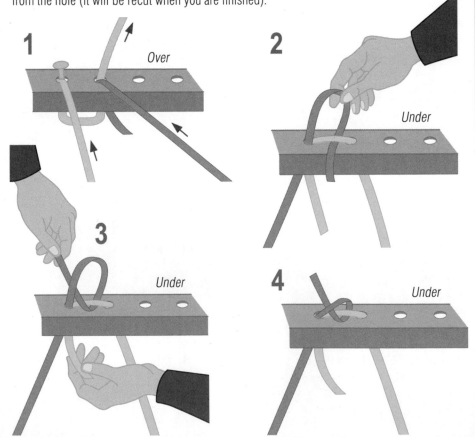

Front corner

ANGLED

Thread the last vertical strand through the second to last hole on the front crosspiece (i.e. through the hole before the corner hole, which should itself stay empty). Thread the strand through the hole on the lateral crosspiece that is directly across from it, so that this strand is parallel to the others **(1)**.

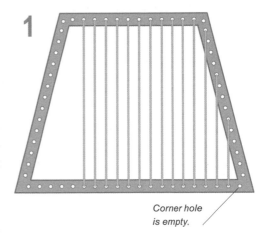

Corner hole
is empty.

ROUNDED

Choose the holes so that the last vertical strand is at an equal distance from the previous strand and the hole on the lateral crosspiece **(2)**.

In all cases, it is normal to have to skip holes on the lateral crosspiece so that all strands are parallel. It is better to join strands on the front crosspiece, since the links underneath are shorter there than on the lateral crosspiece **(3)**.

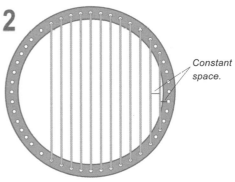

Constant
space.

Remember

Before adding a new strand, always take time to soak it (see page 15). Do not prepare too many strands in advance, especially if it is your first time, since they could dry before you need to use them.

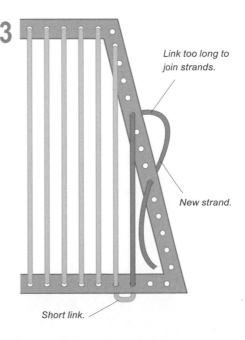

Link too long to
join strands.

New strand.

Short link.

Doubling Strands

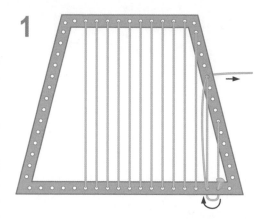

You will double each vertical strand by continuing in the opposite direction with the current cane strand.

STRANDS END ON THE FRONT CROSSPIECE

Pull the strand out of the hole of the second to last vertical strand and double it **(1)**. Secure it with a dowel. Double the last vertical strand, then pull the strand out through the third hole to the right **(2)**.

Continue as such for each hole, in the opposite direction of the first strands, so as to double all of them.

STRANDS END ON THE LATERAL CROSSPIECE

Pull the strand out of the two farthest holes, then go back in the opposite direction to thread it through the skipped hole **(3)**. Secure it with a dowel so it stays tightened. Pull it out through the original hole and double the last vertical strand **(4)**. Then, double each vertical strand in the opposite direction of the first ones. The small cane link visible on the top of the lateral crosspiece will be hidden by the covering strand at the end.

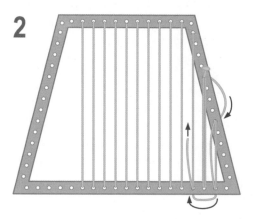

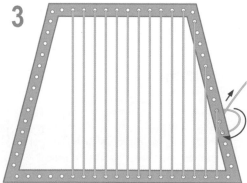

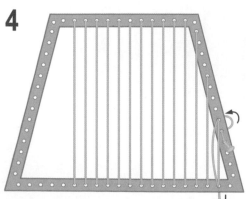

Left side

Once you have come back to where you started, keep tightening vertical strands on the left side of the seat while trying, as much as possible, to work symmetrically on the right side **(1)**.

When you have finished laying the vertical strands on the left side, double them the same way you did for the right side.

When you're done, the strand should be coming out on the left of the starting hole **(2)**.

STRAND POSITION

Throughout the doubling, the two strands should always be side by side, not overlapping. Gently push on the first vertical strand if it interferes with laying the second one.

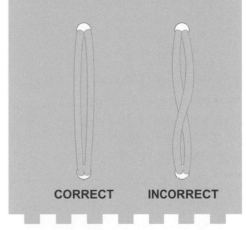

CORRECT   **INCORRECT**

1

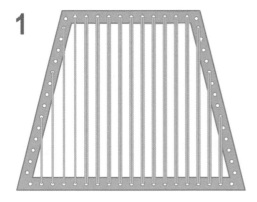

2

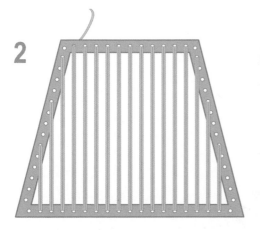

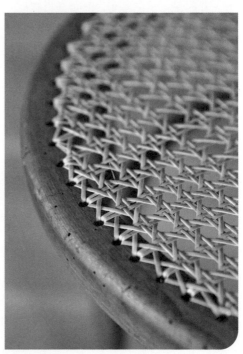

Breaking a Strand in the Middle of Your Work

You can repair this by replacing the broken strand with a small piece of cane.

If the broken strand is not secured on the ends
Leave the holes through which the broken strand passes, but secure the preceding strand's holes with dowels to maintain tension **(1)**.

Pull one of the ends of the broken strand out under the seat to bind it off **(2)**. The end coming out on top will be used to join a new strand.

• Binding off the first end
Turn the seat upside down. Using an awl, carefully raise the link preceding the end of the broken strand **(3)**. Thread the end under the link **(4)**. Repeat this step two or three times so that the end is secured **(5)**. This will be easier if you cut the end at an angle first, so it is tapered.

• Joining the second end
Tie the second end to a new strand (see page 24). Secure the new strand with a dowel, then tighten it by threading it through the corresponding hole. Bind it off using the same method as the first end, under the same link **(6)** or under the next link **(7)**.

If the broken strand is secured at the ends
In this case, since the strand is stuck under a link, there is no need to bind it off. Just make sure it is secured well.

Thread the new strand through the hole and make a knot using a link that already exists. To do this, carefully lift the link with the awl and thread the strand underneath like you would for a regular join **(8)**. Remove the awl: the new strand is secured under the link.

Finish joining by threading the short end of the strand back through the loop **(9)**. Tighten the strand, thread it through the next hole, and secure it with a dowel.

Note
Some seats have a groove underneath to house the links formed by the cane strands (see photo on page 48). When this groove is deep, it is often difficult to lift the links the thread the strands through to bind them off. In this case, pull the strand you are binding off through the top and fasten it with a dowel. Leave the dowel in place until you have to go back through this hole (probably when laying the diagonal strands). The overlapping of the two strands will fully secure the first one.

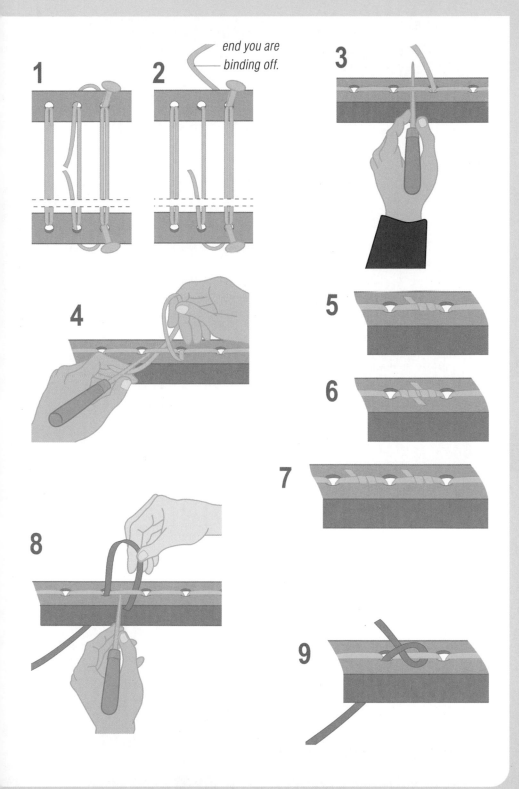

1

2

end you are binding off.

3

4

5

6

7

8

9

Horizontal weaving

This involves horizontally weaving through the vertical strands. You work directly with two strands, moving from the back of the seat to the front.

First row

To Begin

Identify the two holes where you will lay the first horizontal row.

TRAPEZOIDAL SEAT
The first horizontal row goes through the first hole of the lateral crosspieces. Mark these two holes with dowels and make sure that there is the same number of holes between these holes and the bottom on the right and left crosspieces **(1)**.

ROUNDED SEAT
The first horizontal row is stretched between two holes at the rear of the seat. Choose them such that the first row is neither too close nor too far from the crosspiece. The ideal distance will be the same as the one between the first two horizontal rows. Mark your two chosen holes with dowels. Make sure there are the same numbers of holes on either side of the middle **(2)**.

In the hole you have marked on the left, pull out the strand that you finished laying the vertical strands with - this is why we started and finished laying the vertical strands near the left corner. By connecting your work like this, you can avoid binding off the strand for the vertical rows and starting a new one for

the horizontal rows. This principle applies regardless of the shape of the seat.

If, for whatever reason, you don't finish laying the vertical strands in a hole close enough to the first row of horizontal strands, bind off

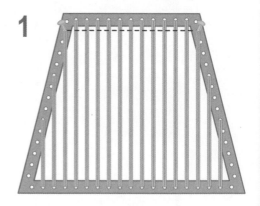

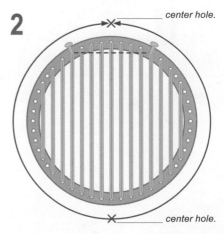

center hole.

center hole.

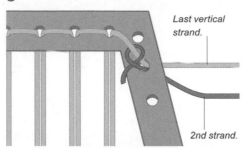

3

Last vertical strand.

2nd strand.

the strand by slipping under a link several times (see figure 5, page 29), then insert a new strand under an existing link on the other side (see figure 8, page 29). Since you're laying the horizontal cane strands directly with two strands, take a new one and soak it.

To start, make a knot using the strand in place as a link **(3)**. The two strands should come out of the same hole **(4)**.

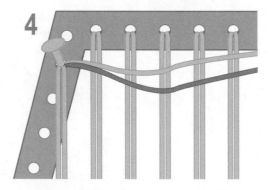

4

Horizontal Strands

Although it is possible to weave the strands with your fingers, a pair of flat needles will make it much easier.

For the purpose of clarity, we'll call the first needle the "shuttle needle" (it weaves) and the second the "running needle" (it holds the rows apart).

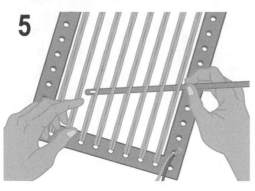

5

FIRST PASS

Run the first needle (shuttle needle) under the first vertical row, over the second one, under the third one, and so on **(5)**. You can go over or under the first vertical row. You can choose the weaving order, as long as you stick to it throughout your work.

At the end of the row, make sure you haven't made any mistakes.

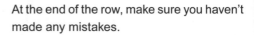

6 Shuttle needle. Running needle.

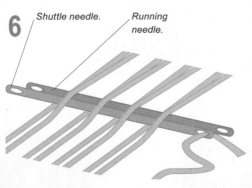

You will use second needle (running needle) to hold apart the vertical rows in order to weave the horizontal rows more quickly. Slide it to the middle of the seat (where there is more give) then, with one hand, turn it a quarter-turn; it will lift up every other vertical row. With the other hand, slip the shuttle needle into the tunnel you just made with the running needle, by passing it over the running needle **(6)**.

When the shuttle needle is in place, release the running needle and slide it to the front of the frame so it doesn't get in the way in the middle of the seat.

Run the end of the first strand through the eye of the shuttle needle. Make sure it is perfectly flat and will not twist. Bend the cane under the needle **(7)**, and then pull the needle so it pulls the cane strand, while using the other hand to keep it from twisting **(8)**.

Tighten the strand, thread it through the corresponding hole on the right crosspiece, and secure it with a dowel.

DOUBLING THE FIRST PASS

Work only with the shuttle needle. Thread the second cane strand through it. Pass it alternatively above and below the vertical rows in the opposite order from the first pass **(9)**. Push it as close as possible to the first, tighten it, thread it through the same hole on the right crosspiece and secure it with a dowel.

7

8

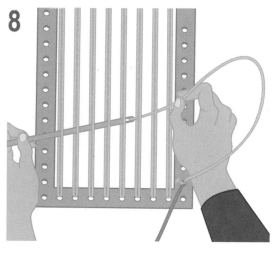

9

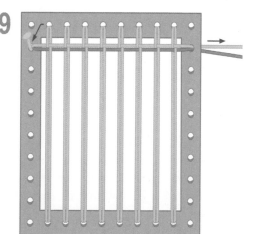

Second row

Pull out the two strands in the hole on right crosspiece you have chosen for the second horizontal row. Secure them in the starting hole with a dowel.

TRAPEZOIDAL SEAT
The second row is placed in the second hole on the lateral crosspieces.

ROUNDED SEAT
Choose the placement of the second row so that you maintain the same distance between the rows.
To do this, it is common to have to skip a hole between the first two rows. Bring the running needle back to the middle of the frame.

If you have to do additional vertical rows on the sides, slide it between them in the order in which they are raised **(1)**.

With the shuttle needle, weave the first strand in the same way as you did the first row: slide the needle through the tunnel made by the running needle, slide the running needle back to the front of the seat, thread the strand through the needle and weave it through, tightening as you go, from one end of the frame to the other **(2)**. Pull the strand out of the hole on the left crosspiece and secure it.

Weave the second strand of the second row with the shuttle needle, making sure to interweave in the opposite direction from the first strand. Make sure you never weave two rows in the same order: this error is irreversible.

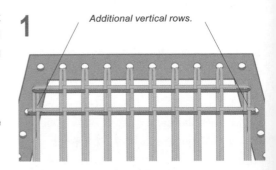

1 *Additional vertical rows.*

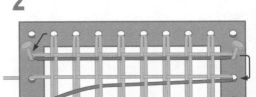

2

Remaining rows

Continue in the same way, making sure to tighten the strands at the end of each row to keep them straight.

Combing

After several rows, start retightening the rows two at a time using the comb. The goal is to have straight and evenly spaced rows. For straightening and tightening to be effective, you need to moisten the cane with a sponge.

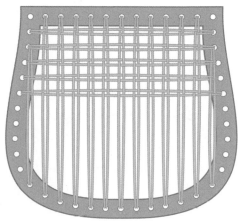

CORRECT

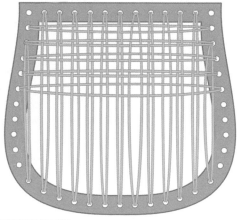

INCORRECT

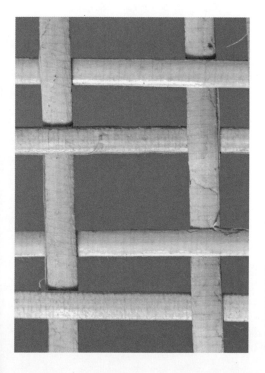

Remember

When one of the two strands ends, join a new one as you normally would (see page 24).

Last rows

When you have woven the horizontal rows through about two-thirds of the frame, you will notice that it starts to get difficult to turn the running needle because of the strand tension. Do not force it, because you could crack the vertical rows. Remove the running needle from the frame and keep working with just the shuttle needle.

As you continue, when you start to have difficulty using the shuttle needle without risk of breaking the vertical strands, continue weaving by hand.

This last part takes longer, but if you wet the strands to soften them, you should not have any difficulty interweaving them.

The last horizontal row should not be too far from or too close to the edge of the frame. On a trapezoidal seat, it is located in the last hole before the corner **(1)**. On a round seat, continue to maintain the spacing between rows until you get close to the crosspiece **(2)**.

Final combing

When you are done laying the horizontal cane strands, moisten the cane again with a sponge, then retighten the two strands of each row with the comb, just like you did throughout this step. Repeat this on the vertical rows, too, to get a clean grid.

Remember

Combing only works correctly if the cane is moist enough. Be careful not to break the cane by handling it too roughly.

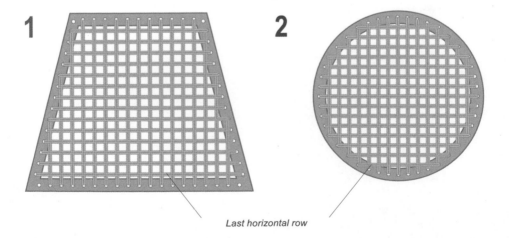

Last horizontal row

Diagonal weaving

Now you will weave the cane strands diagonally through the vertical and horizontal strands.
For the diagonal strands, you will use cane that is wider than the cane for the horizontal strands, but you will not double it.

To Begin

Start laying the diagonal strands from a corner on the front of the seat, on the side where you ended the last horizontal row.

TRAPEZOIDAL SEAT

Pull both strands of the horizontal row out of the hole on the corner of the frame **(1)**. Use them to join the strand for weaving the diagonal rows (see page 24).

SEAT ROUNDED AT THE FRONT

Pull both strands of the last horizontal row out of one of the two holes next to the one they are in, staying as close as possible to the corner hole if you can't actually reach it **(2)**.

CIRCULAR SEAT

Start the first diagonal row in the hole next to the one in which the two strands of the last horizontal row are located.

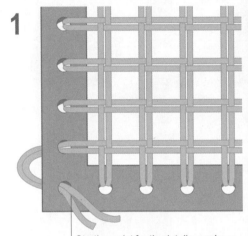

Starting point for the 1st diagonal row

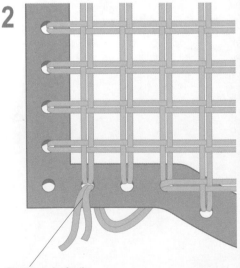

Starting point for the 1st diagonal row

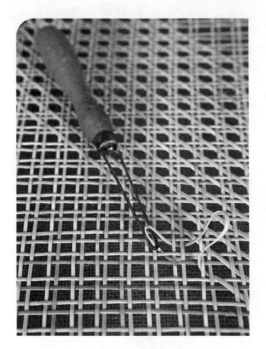

first horizontal strand above and then below the vertical strands, or by weaving the first horizontal row below and then above the vertical rows.

FIRST CASE

If the first strand of each horizontal row goes, from left to right, below the first vertical row then below the second, the southwest/northeast diagonal row should go above the vertical strands and below the horizontal strands. In the diagram below **(1)**, the blue circles show correct interweaving. The diagonal strand should slide easily under the horizontal strand where it meets the vertical strands.

To understand the principle, experiment a bit by inverting the weave with a left over strand of cane.

You will see that the diagonal set up twists itself and is caught every time it reaches an intersection point where the vertical and horizontal weave meet **(2)**..

If you start the first diagonal row in the left front corner, it will cross the seat diagonally towards the right rear corner. It probably will not land there exactly, unless the frame is perfectly square. In all cases, there is no need to calculate from the beginning which hole the diagonal strand will end up in. It will automatically make its way by passing alternatively above and below the cane that is already in place, and the strand will end up in the right hole.

Weave direction

There are two possible directions:
• passing above a pair of vertical strands and below a pair of horizontal strands;
• passing below a pair of vertical strands and above a pair of horizontal strands;
The direction you should choose for laying the vertical strands depends on how you laid the horizontal strands, either by weaving the

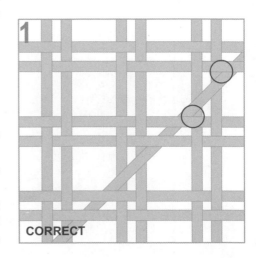

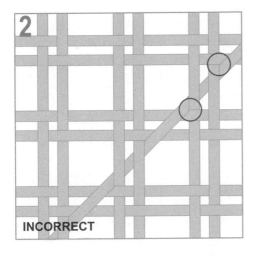

INCORRECT

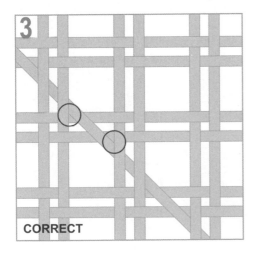

CORRECT

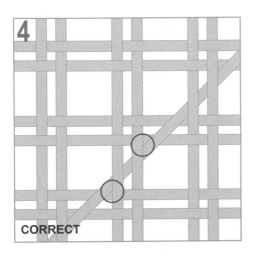

CORRECT

CANE SLIDE DIRECTION

For weaving the diagonal rows, it is useful to identify the slide direction of the cane. You will notice, if you run your finger in one direction along the length of the strand, the various nodes will be rough and in the other direction, they will be smooth.

Take the cane in the direction where it is smooth and slide your finger to its end and join this end to the previous strand. This way, the cane will easily slide through the weave.

Therefore, it is important that you don't make a mistake when starting to lay the vertical strands. Incorrectly laying the diagonal strands, besides making the work more difficult, inevitable leads to rapid wear and tear of the cane.

The southeast/northwest diagonal will go conversely above the horizontal rows and below the vertical rows **(3)**.

SECOND CASE

If the first strand of each horizontal row goes, from left to right, below the first vertical row and then above the second, the southwest/northeast diagonal row should go above the horizontal rows and below the vertical rows **(4)**.

Laying the first SW/NE diagonal row

Once you have determined the weave direction of the first diagonal row based on the horizontal and vertical rows, weave it through the frame. In the two cases shown on 40-41 the route taken by the woven diagonal could be compared to a small stairway.

Cut the end of the cane strand on the diagonal. With the tip of the awl, pull it up like you would to curl the ribbon on a gift box. Once threaded into a hole in the weave, the curled strand will come on its own out of the next hole, without you having to get hold of it under the seat.

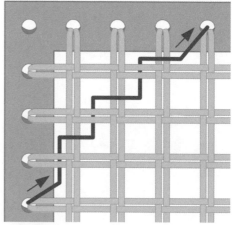

1ˢᵗ CASE

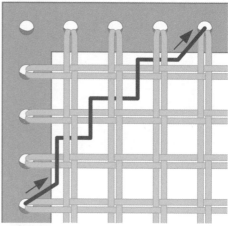

2ⁿᵈ CASE

FYI

Instead of curling the end of the strand, you can use a wire caning tool (see photo opposite).
This little tool brings the cane out to the top of the seat, meaning that you don't have to have a hand permanently under the frame.

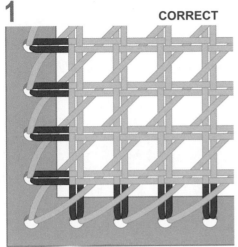

1 CORRECT

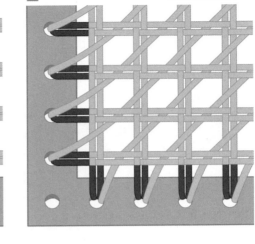

2 INCORRECT

Once you have woven about 7 cm of diagonal strands, pull the whole length of the cane strand while stretching it. You will actually be unable to tighten it properly if you wait to pull it until the end of the diagonal row.

While laying the diagonal cane strands, carefully wipe down the cane with a dry cloth before using it. If you use it straight out of the water, when it is very wet, it will be very difficult to pull it without making it grate against the cane and it will be more likely to break. Once you wipe it down, it will slide more easily when weaving.

If the cane is flexible enough, use it as is without soaking it.

To make the cane slide more easily, you can even coat the back of it with paraffin before putting it in place. This method is especially effective when weaving tightly.

Weaving around the edges

The difficulty In laying the diagonal strands is that the diagonal rows must be as straight as possible. However, this is not a problem once you have gotten started correctly, since the stepped path is determined by the vertical and horizontal strands.

The really difficult area is at the ends of the diagonal rows. People often hesitate between two holes when the cane strand does not seem to be properly placed in either one.

In order to avoid errors, keep in mind a little rule that will give you straight diagonal rows and an aesthetic finish on the edge of the frame. This rule involves continuing to stick to the stepped path until the ends of the vertical and horizontal rows. In the diagrams above, these ends are in blue to show the concept. If the blue part is large enough for the diagonal to continue on its way, the strand should be woven before it is threaded into the next hole in the frame **(1)**. If you don't follow this rule, your cane work will have a rather sloppy aspect **(2)**.

Laying the other SW/NE diagonal rows

Weave the diagonal rows the same way, working alternately from front to back and back to front. Cover the rest of the seat like this so as to arrive at the corner of the frame.

Start a new strand where you had started laying the first half of the diagonal cane strands. Weave the second half working as you did the first half.

The curves

The holes in the frame that receive two diagonals are called "curves" **(1)**. All corner holes are automatically curves. The number of curves depends on the shape of the frame. On a perfectly square seat, there are only four corner holes; on a round seat, there are many.

By respecting the stairway path of each diagonal you will easily see which holes will become curves.

A curve on one side of the frame will match a skipped hole on the other side of the frame **(2)**.

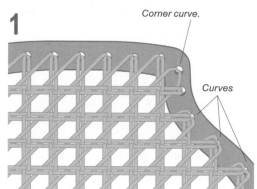

1

Corner curve.

Curves

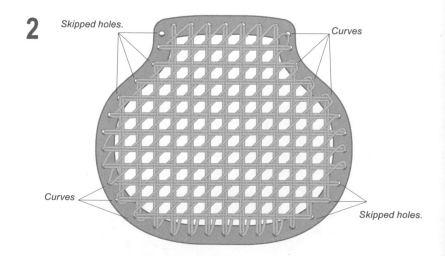

2

Skipped holes.

Curves

Curves

Skipped holes.

By definition it is impossible to finish one diagonal and begin the next in the same hole, because the cane won't be blocked under the frame. Therefore you should proceed in the following manner. Bring the cane out in the next hole and weave a diagonal: the second diagonal curve is skipped **(3)**.

At the return of the cane, weave the skipped diagonal, thread the cane into the center hole, and then bring it out skipping a hole **(4)**.

With a circular seat, you will often have to repeat this operation because the curves are often very close to each other.

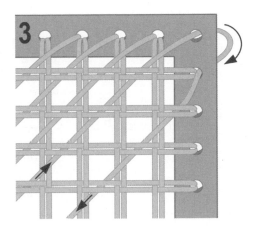
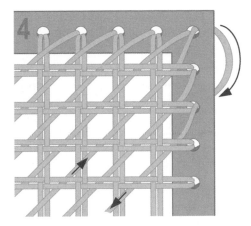

Laying the SE/NW diagonal rows

When you have finished weaving the diagonals southwest/northeast, do the diagonals southeast/northwest.

Work in exactly the same way, but reversing the order of weave. Firstly, pass the center diagonal then on both sides, cover the two halves of the seat one after the other.

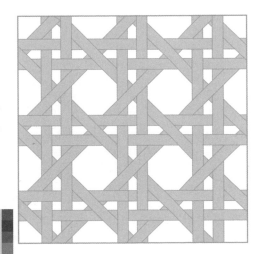

Tip

Imagine the stairway path the cane takes (for example "on the verticals, under the horizontals"). When you reach the frame, ask yourself: "Do I pass on the last vertical part or under the last horizontal part?"

Binding

This last stage of weaving consists of fixing a larger cane than the two previous ones, all around the frame to hide the holes.

This method of finishing is recent, so therefore wasn't used in the past. It isn't necessary to do any binding if the original chair didn't have one. However, it is necessary to work very carefully at the edge of the caning (see page 43).

Cane size

You will need two types of cane:
• a strand of 3.5mm wide (length = the frame's perimeter + 10cm security margin);
• A few strands of 1.8 or 2mm wide, chosen from amongst the longest in the hank or coil.

Preparation

With a pointed pair of scissors, cut the little extremities of cane close to the holes on top of the frame. Using an awl, make sure that all the holes are clear.

Soak the cane you are going to use. It should be very supple, therefore very damp, to make working easier. Count on soaking for about a quarter of an hour.

The binding's starting point must be on the back crosspiece, in any hole apart from the corner ones. You can start by joining the binder to the last diagonal done (see page 24).

If you didn't do it as you went along the weave, bind off all the other strands under the seat (see pages 28-29).

Stitching the wide cane

Start off with the finest strands of cane in the chosen hole, by joining it with the diagonal that hasn't been bound off or by using one of the bridges under the frame.

During binding, it won't be possible to use dowels, so you must keep the tension by hand. Keep the join well tightened.

Thread the strand into the starting hole once more to form a loop on top of the frame (1)..

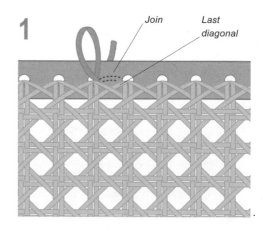

1

Join   Last diagonal

Thread the largest strands through the loop, leaving its extremity overlapping the preceding hole. Pull on the loop so that it lies tight against the wood (2).

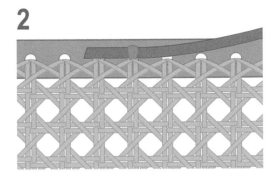

Wedge the frame vertically between your knees – the underside on your right if you are right-handed, or on the left if you are left-handed. This posture will allow you to make sure that the cane is correctly placed on both sides of the frame.

Bend the fine strand in two under the frame. Bring it out of the following hole, tightening it well. Thread the large strand into the loop formed on the top. Tighten the loop to block the large strand. Bend the fine strand once more under the frame, bring it out of the following hole to form another loop, and thread the large strand into it. Continue in the same way from hole to hole (3).

Cut

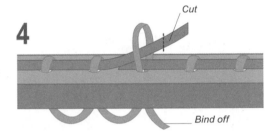

Bind off

It is important to keep the fine cane tight to get a neat finish.

Joins

Once the strand is finished, join it normally by making a knot with another strand of the same size. When the binding is finished, cut the little extremities of the knots close to the top of the seat.

FYI

It is essential to keep the fine strand well tightened to get a neat finish.

Corners

When you reach the corner holes, bend the large strand so that it matches the shape of the frame. Make sure that it is damp enough not to break where you bend it.

Binding off the two strands

Once you reach the starting point again, make sure that the two extremities of the large strand overlap each other. Bind off the fine strand under the frame by twisting it two or three times under a bridge, then cut the surplus close to the cane.

Finishing

Once you have finished caning your seat, you should verify your work to make sure that it will be long-lasting. After that you are free to choose the finish: natural, tinted ceruse or painted.

Final repairs

Closely examine the reverse side of the caning. Cut all the sticking out strands close to the weave. If some of them are badly stopped, glue them with a little wood-glue or block them with small wooden dowels pushed into the holes concerned. (You can use pegs sold for assembling furniture).

Tinting

Raw cane is almost white. You can tint it giving it a patina aspect with products especially made for this effect. It is also possible to ceruse it or, to give it a modern style, to paint it. In each case, there are products to protect it.

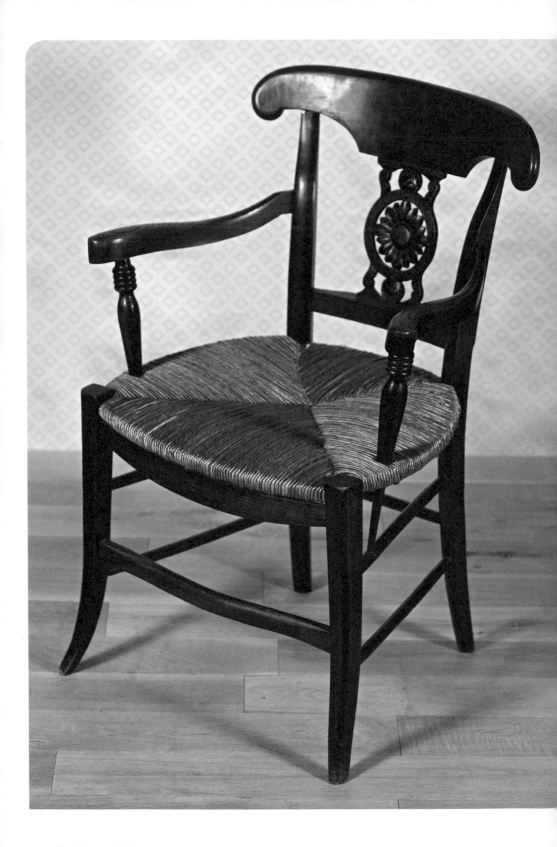

Reseating

You will learn the technical basics through three examples:
a square stool, a rectangular stool and a chair which, by
definition, has a more or less pronounced trapezoid form.
The explications are concentrated on the seat,
but the technique is identical for chair-backs.

Material

From natural straw to synthetics fibers, through cord and recycled paper, you have a vast range of choice when it comes to giving a new lease of life to your chairs.

A lot of different material can be used to reseat a chair. How to choose between natural straw (marsh grass, rye straw, rush, sea grass, raffia), synthetic material or recycled paper cords sold by the meter? It all depends on both the style you want to give to your chair and on your own skill. Your first results might leave a lot to be desired, but with a little patience you will eventually master the techniques.

The best way to start is by using marsh grass. This material helps you to fully understand traditional reseating by discovering its knacks, its possibilities and its limits. You will feel more at ease when it comes to using other materials, whether they are simpler or more complex to use. This is why all the explanations in this book are based on using marsh grass.

MARSH GRASS

With its pale green/gold color, it has a rustic aspect. It is a grass of the Carex family. Depending on the species and the regions where it grows, it is also called "sedge" or "saw grass". Sun-dried straw has lovely gold or copper tints. Specialist suppliers offer marsh grass in different packaging: from 5kg bundles to 50kg bales.

RYE STRAW

This is blonder and glossier than marsh grass and is called "golden straw ". It is often used to wrap straw threads to give them a more sophisticated finish or to add a touch of color here and there. It is sold in a large number of tints, from "old metal" to florescent colors. Rye straw is used in exactly the same way as marsh grass, but it is delicate and tedious work as you should wrap it round each strand as you go along.

TWISTED STRAW

These are ready-made twisted strands, which save you having to make them yourself and from having to check on their solidity while you use them. They are often made from seagrass wrapped in rye straw. Although they are great in a practical sense, they offer neither the charm nor the quality of traditional straw.

ALTERNATIVE MATERIAL

Raffia, synthetic cord, recycled fibers, paper twists... every day the market offers new products that can be used for reseating chairs. Their colors and textures are often seductive, so experiment with them to discover their potentials.

Handling

You need about 1kg of rush to reseat a chair. Threads measure about 120cm in length, and their width varies according to the bundle. Straw can be kept for several years if it is kept in a cool, well-aired place, safe from damp which will make it rot.

Dry rush is liable to split or break, so handle it carefully. Always handle it from its largest end otherwise you will break it. For this reason, bundles should always be stacked in the same direction, with the thickest part on one end and the tips on the other.

Soaking

You should always work with damp rush because it is easier to use when it is supple. The best way is to immerse it without bending it, into a large tub of cold water. Soaking time depends on the bundle and on the size of the threads (the larger they are, the longer they need to be soaked). Count on soaking them around a quarter of an hour; after that rush swells and then gets slack when it dries out. After 10 minutes, if you find it supple enough to work with, don't wait any longer.

If you haven't got a large enough tub to soak the entire threads, start off by soaking the larger end and then bend the rest of the threads so that they are under water. Do this carefully to avoid breaking the threads while making sure that they are all immersed.

Only soak the smallest amount possible that you will use at any given time; although it is possible, it is not recommended that you wet and re-wet the rush strands multiple times.

For the first session, soak a small handful of strands as you work, and add more as you need them.

Once the rush has soaked and is supple enough to work with, remove it from the water and place it on a damp cloth.

Maintenance

For the general up-keep of your rush seats, dust them regularly with a supple silk-brush, being careful to respect the direction of the fibers and the weave. If they are really dirty, clean them with warm salted water (five soup spoons of cooking salt for 1 liter of water) and then leave them to dry in a moderately warm room out of direct sunlight. You can always give them an extra shine by cleaning them with lemon juice added to warm water

INSTALLATION AND POSITION

Set your working space up in a room where it doesn't matter if the floor gets wet or dirty. Put the damp rush on a damp piece of cloth which will soak up the surplus water.

Solidary frame
It's best to sit on a low chair so that you have the rush close to hand. Place the bundle on the side you are comfortable with (right or left hand); the thickest ends beside you (because you should always pick up a thread by its thickest end). Set the chair you want to reseat in front of you and grip it between your knees to keep it from moving.

Embedded frame
This should be dismantled and fixed to a bench (see page 59).

Tip

At the end of each session, remember to collect up the scraps of rush and dry them outside (in a cage for example). You will need them for padding the seat when you reach the end of your work.

Tools

A chair bottomer's tools are simple and not too expensive. A part from specific items such as the tamping iron and the packing tool, you probably already have the necessary tools at home.

TAMPING IRON (1)

This tool, either iron or wooden, comprises a long tapering part and a perpendicular handle. If you can't find one, you can eventually use a large wooden spoon.

PACKING TOOL (2)

About 20cm long, this tool is a flat piece of polished wood or steel, pointed at one end and rounded at the other. It can be replaced by a paper-knife or a bone folder.

You will also need:
• a tub large enough the soak the rush — the bathtub for example;
• a tape measure;
• a Stanley knife or box cutter;
• a large pair of scissors;
• a small pair of pliers;
• a few clothes pegs;
• string;
• clamps if you are working on an embedded frame (see page 59).

Note

If there are no specialized shops near you, look for suppliers on the Internet. You can also ask antique dealers or furniture restorers for advice. However, you might find yourself having to make some of your own tools!

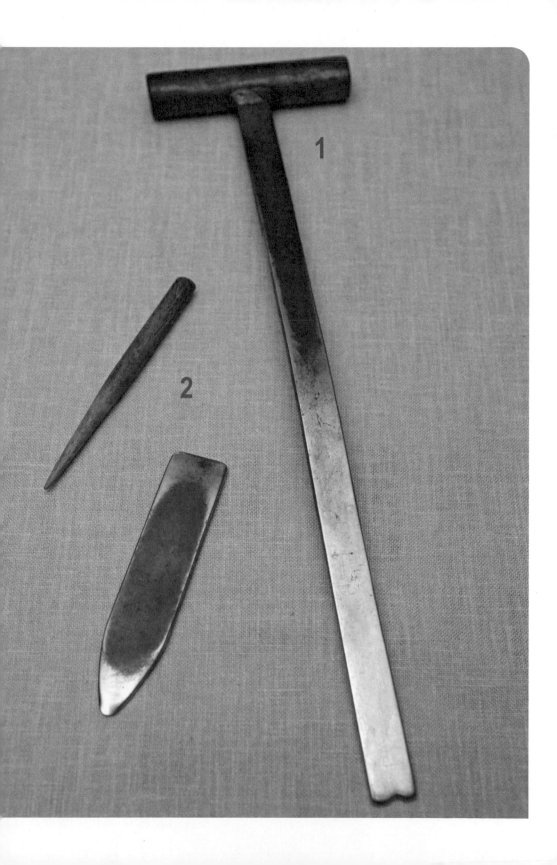

Preparing the seat

As in any craft work, preparation is an essential step. Take time to prepare your seat properly to enhance the future reseating.

Old rush

Cut away and get rid of the old rush using a pair of scissors or a Stanley knife. Don't bother to keep any of it as old rush isn't good for anything. Make sure you get all the bits stuck in the crosspieces and between the uprights.

Straw guard

As their name suggests, rush guards are used to protect the edges when reseating a chair. Some chairs don't have them; others have them in front or on each side. Removing them can be difficult as the wood — often very dry — risks splitting or breaking. Proceed in the following manner: Remove the rush wedged behind the guard by pulling the strands one by one. A gap will appear between the crosspiece and the guard. Gently press the guard against the crosspiece (it is flexible enough for this) to bring out the nails towards the front. Remove these with the pliers. Lift the guard out of the notches that keep it in place in the chair-legs.

Repairing

Reseating should be done on a chair that is in good condition. Once the old rush is removed, verify the structure's stability. Before starting on the work, do any necessary repairs using fast drying wood glue and leave it to dry out completely before starting on the reseating.

rush-guard

Solidary seat or embedded frame?

Most of the time chairs have solidary seats – attached to the legs and these can't be taken apart. In this case you will notice that the lateral crosspieces aren't necessarily at the same level as those at the front and at the back, but slightly higher, for reasons in the way they were manufactured. Certain professional chair bottomers fix the chair to a vice set on a tripod so that they can work standing up, at a desired height. Apart from being hard to find, this item isn't really very practical for beginners.

However, certain chairs are made with an embedded frame that is fixed to an apron. You should be able to pull the frame out sim-

ply by pushing beneath the chair. If the frame is screwed to the apron, simply remove or spread the rush to have access to the screws. Fix the frame to a table using a clamp to stop it from moving around while you are working. The work is carried out in the same way as a solidary seat.

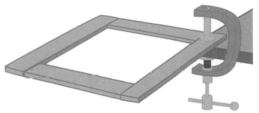

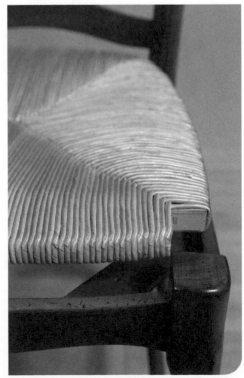

Square stool

This is the easiest seat to replace. A square stool is a perfect support for learning all the basic techniques and to acquire the essential knacks.

Making a strand

A strand is made by twisting rush threads. It is wrapped around the crosspieces and it alone forms the seat. You use the same strand throughout the work adding threads when necessary.

The strand must be perfectly even. Its diameter depends on the number of threads you choose at the beginning. For your first seat it's best to avoid a strand that is too thin – this would take longer and be more difficult. It is better to choose a somewhat rustic-looking but successful result, with a strand of 6 to 10mm.

The number of threads that make up a strand varies according to their size. Take a small fistful of threads. Twist them as if you were trying to wring them out. Try out different numbers of threads until you get the diameter you want to work with.

Starting loop

Once you have finished the previous step, flatten out your threads and place them on the back crosspiece against the left corner (as a square stool has neither back nor front, you can start on whichever side you decide is the back).

Pass 15cm of them (the thickest ends) under the crosspiece while flattening them on top to avoid them being too thick **(1)**. Twisting them, gather the thick ends under the crosspiece and the longer strands above it.

Twist the strand to make sure the thick ends are blocked in the long ends **(2)**: turn the strand two or three times in succession on itself, using the same wrist movement as winding up a clock. Smooth it on all the length so that the points don't get tangled in the opposite direction.

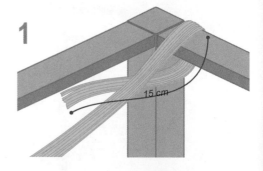

15 cm

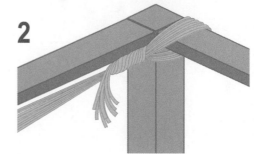

Just before completely hiding the thick ends in the strand, separate the long threads into two: A consisting of long threads, B consisting of long threads and the thick ends **(3)**.

Twist A tightly around B in a way to wedge the thick end in the strand **(4)**. The loop should be solidly fixed to the crosspiece so that it doesn't come undone under tension. It doesn't matter if it doesn't look very nice, because it will be hidden under the rush, but it must be resistant.

Continue to twist the longest threads to make the strand: do another couple of turns and then smooth out the rush all along its length (this operation must be repeated throughout the work).

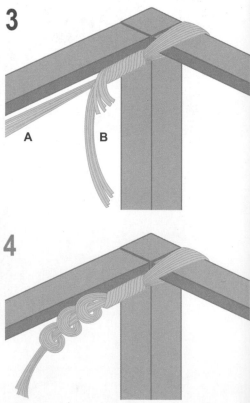

3

A   B

4

As soon as the strand starts to get thin add inside one or two new threads (thickest end first). To do this, slightly part the threads to be able to slip in the new threads among them so that they are hidden in the middle of the strand **(5)** the carry on twisting the rush normally.

5

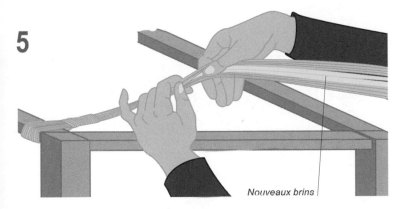

Nouveaux brins

Rules to respect

- Add rush whenever necessary to avoid the strand becoming too thin. Don't hesitate adding a new thread every 5cm. It is better to add threads little by little and often. If you wait until the strand is very thin and then add a lot of new threads together, your work will be lumpy and uneven.
- Twist enough threads so that they stay together, but not too many because the strand would become deformed and the threads would break. A lot of beginners have a tendency to add a lot of threads because they think it will make the seat stronger.
- Don't separate the strand in two parts twisted round each other, twist all the threads together.

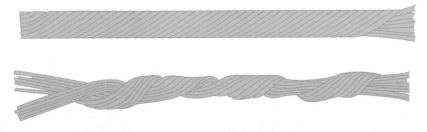

First round

First corner

To make things easier, the crosspieces are named from A to D from the left-hand crosspiece and taking a counter clockwise direction **(1)**. The starting loop was done on crosspiece D (see page 60).

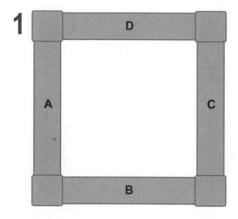

Make a strand long enough to wrap round crosspiece B with an extra 30cm or so. Pass the strand over B, bring it out on the underside of the crosspiece, pass it on A and bring it out again on the interior in the direction of corner C/B **(2)**.

After you have formed the corner, pack the strand close against the leg's wood with your thumb **(3)**. Check the part of the strand under the seat: it should also be packed close against the leg's wood.

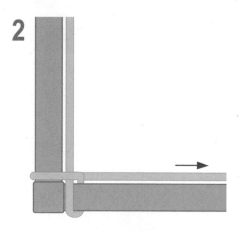

From the start, keep them at an angle of 90°, without worrying about the small hole which forms at the intersection: it will become invisible as the work advances. It the stool's legs are round, don't make the corner too tight because the rush will automatically marry the foot's curve **(4 and 5)**.

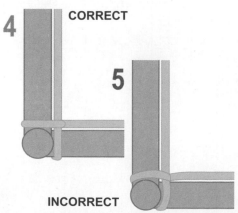

CORRECT

INCORRECT

Following corners

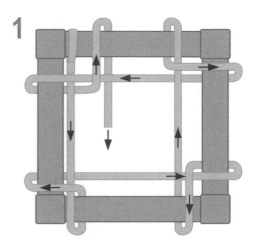

Proceed in the same way (1). Turn the stool so that you can pull the strand that has just formed the following corner towards you with all your strength. As you direct the strand from one corner to another don't hesitate to pull it has hard as you can, because when dry the rush will loosen along its length and its thickness will retract. Successful reseating depends on the strand's tension. You just need to moderate it a little at the corners so that they are right angles.

SECOND CORNER

Pass the strand on crosspiece C and bring it out on the interior of the seat. Form an angle by passing on B. Bring the strand out on the interior in the direction of corner C/D. Turn the stool to tighten the strand.

THIRD CORNER

Pass the strand on crosspiece D and bring it out on the underside of the seat. Form the angle by passing on C. Bring it out on the interior in the direction of corner D/A.

FOURTH CORNER

Pass the strand on crosspiece A and bring it out on the interior of the seat. Form the angle by passing on D. Place the strand on the starting loop to hide it. You have finished the first round.

Tip

Don't forget to vigorously tighten the strand all the time so that the angles don't get deformed.

Following rounds

Continue in the same way for the following rounds, packing the strands tightly against each other at every round. The strands under the seat should be packed as tightly as those on top. After every fifth round or so, make sure that the corners are perfect right-angles. To do this, attach the strand to the stool's lower bar with a clothes peg **(1)**. Measure the space between the corners of the seat's circumference; you should find the same in the centre **(2)**. If you have made the strand evenly and have kept up the same tension, packing the strands close together at each round, the spaces should be equal. However you might encounter one of the two following problems:

CORNERS WITH ACUTE ANGLES (3)

You didn't pull the strand hard enough when you were making the corners. With your thumb, try to push the inner part of the corner towards the leg.

CORNERS WITH OBTUSE ANGLES (4)

Retighten each round of strand one against the other on the circumference of the seat by pushing them with the flat part of the packing tool until you get neat right-angles **(5)**.

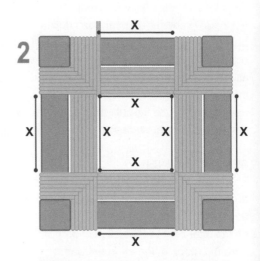

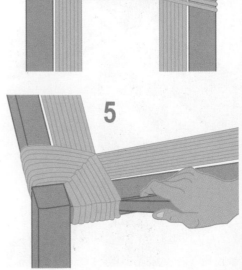

Taking a break

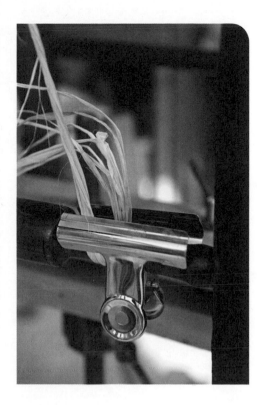

Tightening

1

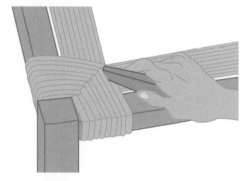

Once you have moved a little forward in your work, leave it to dry for a while (at least a day), then pack the rounds of strands with the flat part of the packing tool to make more space at the seat's center (see fig 5 on the previous page). Don't just tighten the seat's periphery, because the angles would deform. Pack the underside of the corners too, at the intersections, to keep them at right-angles (1).

As firmly as possible, pack the first round of strand closely against the leg, then pack the second round against the first and so on. Don't hesitate to squash the rounds tight against each other, being careful that they don't overlap and making sure that you don't damage them with the end of the packing tool.

Note

The flat part of the packing tool should be sharp so that it can easily slide between the rounds of strands. If necessary, sharpen it with sandpaper.

Always slide the packing tool progressively from the centre towards the exterior **(2)**. If you do the opposite you will be going "against the pile" and you risk damaging the strand. Repeat the tightening operation on the two sides of the four corners in an even way.

When you have finished, make sure that the distance between the corners is the same and that the angles are straight **(3)**

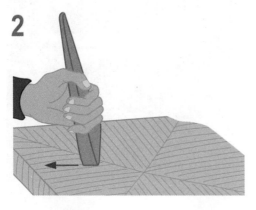

2

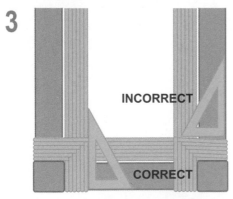

3

INCORRECT

CORRECT

Tip

It is normal for the strand to break from time to time: it shows that you are pulling it hard enough. Undo about 50 cm of it and remake it by adding threads as you do during the normal course of your work.

Last rounds

When the hole in the center gets smaller and smaller, you'll need to pay close attention to make sure that you form the corners without making a mistake. Keep the working order fixed in your mind: firstly corner A, then corner B, C and lastly D **(4)**.

When you start having difficulties pushing the strand through the center hole, enlarge it slightly with the point of the packing tool **(5)** pull on the folded strand with the help of a metal hook (or caning needle if you have one) **(6)**.

Make sure that the rounds on the underside aren't overlapping. They should be progressing in the same way and with the same number as the topside.

When you can no longer push the strand through the center hole, leave the seat to dry out for at least two or three days. Then you will see that the rush has retracted again. It will be possible to pack the rounds again and add a few others.

Padding

Once the work is finished, and while it is drying out, you will start on the padding. This rather tedious operation consists of slipping small plugs of rush into the underside of the seat to give it volume while retightening the strands.

Place the stool upside-down on a table, the legs towards the ceiling. Put the scraps of rush you have kept for this purpose within hand's reach. Make sure that they are very dry (damp rush will rot). Pad the sides in the following manner.

4

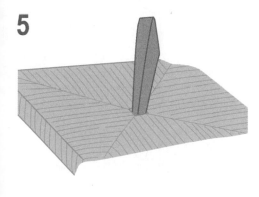

5

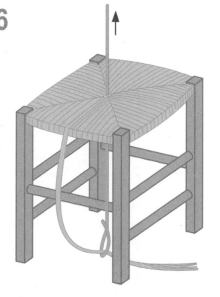

6

VARIANT

- - - - - - - - - - - - - - -

Padding is done intentionally at the end of the work, because it is at this moment that the tension is more even. However, it is quite common to see chair-bottomers pad out the seats as they go along, because it is easier to slip in the plugs under the weave. They generally proceed in three steps: they weave a third of the seat and then pad it; they weave the second third and then pad it; they weave the last third and pad it. Although it is a practical way to work, this technique can lead to irregularities, especially when you are a beginner.

Count from six to eight rounds from one of the stool's legs, or from one corner of the frame. Lift them with the tamping iron to form a pocket.

Make a small plug with the scraps of rush by rolling them in your hands, making sure that you don't cut yourself. Slip it into the pocket made by the tamping iron. To pack it completely, push it as far as possible towards the leg or corner with the end of the tamping iron.

Repeat this until the pocket is as hard as wood.

Count another six to eight rounds after the padded part. Pad with small plugs, packing carefully so that you get an even density.

Continue to work from the leg or corner towards the center until all the first half of the first side is well padded.

Pad the second half of the first side in the same way, proceeding from the leg or corner towards the center. Finish padding the first half by the middle **(7)**.

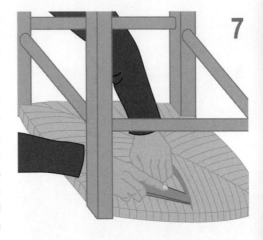

Press firmly down on the padded part to make sure that it isn't possible to add any more rush. You should try to introduce the maximum number of small plugs to obtain a hard seat. Make sure that none of the rounds on the underside of the seat are buried in the padding. Once the four sides are padded in the same way, you will notice that the rush has retightened.

Put the stool back on its feet. Do a general tightening on all the rounds, starting with the corners. With the flat part of the packing tool, pack the rounds towards the corners, taking them one by one, to make another bit of space in the center. At the same time, smooth them out from the center towards the edges, making sure that they don't overlap.

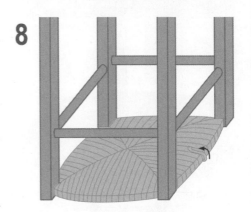

If you find that some of them are overlapping, it's probably because they are less tight or a little bigger that their neighbor; press them down to lay them next to the others. On the other hand, if a round has slipped under another, it is perhaps because the strand is thinner at this point: bring it back up with the packing tool so that it retakes its place alongside the next round.

Once you have put each round in its proper place, you will almost certainly have made enough space to add one or two more. Detach the strand (which should be attached to the lower bar of the stool with a clothes peg), re-dampen it and do the number of rounds necessary until there is only a tiny space in the center. It is absolutely essential that the rounds are properly packed together

because, without mentioning the unaesthetic aspect the stool will have, they will rub together and fray very quickly.

Finishing

Let the work rest for a week, then check to see if it is possible to add more padding or do another round. To finish off definitely the strand, slip it under the seat inside the padding, directly below the last round. Push it with the tamping iron to make sure it is firmly jammed in **(8)**. To finish off, cut all the little "beards" sticking out of the strands with a sharp pair of scissors.

Rectangular stool

The general principle is the same as for a square stool. The major difference is creating the center part, made thanks to eight-cane weaving. Fix the starting loop to the extreme left of the large crosspiece at the back of the stool, in the same way as for a square stool **(1)**.

Be sure to keep the angles straight by vigorously tightening the strand. Measure the rounds: you should get the same distance X between corners A/B and C/D; and the same distance Y between the corners D/A and B/C **(2)**.

Continue until the short crosspieces are completely covered with well tightened rounds. Before filling in the large space that remains in the center, make sure that you can't add another round or so on the short crosspieces because after eight-cane weaving it won't be possible to correct them.

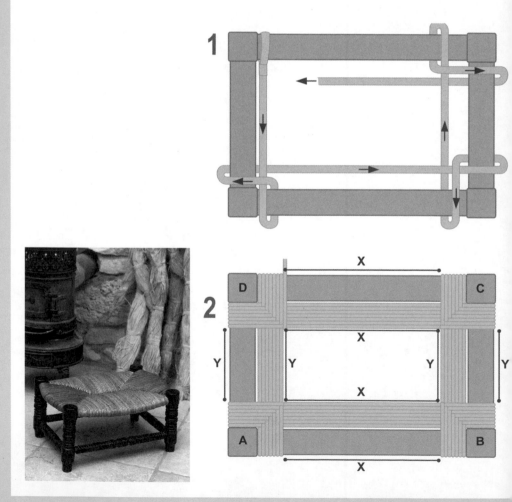

Padding the short sides

The rush should be left to dry for a few days before starting on the eight-cane weave. During this time pad the short sides so that they are very hard. Tighten the rounds against each other, pushing them towards the corners to get enough space to add another round or two.

Eight-cane weaving

Once the short sides are definitively finished, start the eight-cane weaving. Start from the place you have finished covering the short sides — for example, the right-hand side. Pass the weave successively over then under the back long crosspiece and bring it out in the center; pass it over and the under the front long crosspiece and bring it out in the centre, and so on **(3)**.

Progress towards the left (if you have started on the right,) or towards the right (if you have started on the left). Don't hesitate to squash the strands close together, both in the center and on the edges of the seat.

Padding the long sides

Once the eight-cane weaving is finished, leave it to dry for a few days. During this time completely pad the long sides. Tighten the rounds by packing them one by one against each other to gain a space to add an extra round or two. When you are sure that you can't add any more rounds, finish by sliding the strand under the seat inside the padding (see fig 2, page 70)..

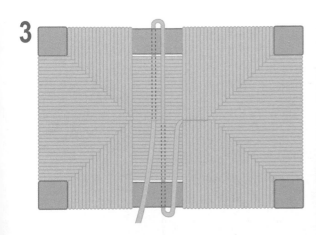

Chair

With chairs, the difficulty arises with the fact that the back crosspiece is always shorter than the front crosspiece, whlch gives the chair seat a trapezoid shape.

If you proceed in the same way as with a stool, by turning evenly to form the corners, the back of the chair will be finished, while there will be a large space at the front. This is why you should begin by filling the front two corners until you get the same length between the front and back crosspieces.

Once you have re-established a "square", you can continue as with a stool. There are two methods for re-establishing a square: the loop method and the two-strand method.

Loop method

This is commonly used and is recommended for beginners as it is very simple. It consists of working solely on the front of the chair until a square is re-established **(1)**.

Forming the loop

Use enough rush to make a strand twice as thick as a strand used for a stool. The starting loop should be very solid because you will be attaching other strands on to it.

Place the tuft of rush flat on the back crosspiece, against the left-hand corner. Leave about 20cm of thick ends hanging free **(2)**..

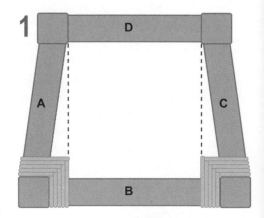

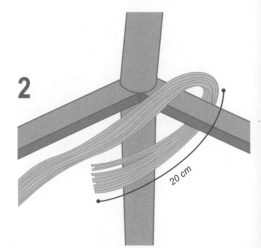

Twist the large ends with the rush on top to form a loop of a length about equal to a third of the side crosspiece **(3)**.

Before hiding the large ends in the strand, consolidate the loop by dividing the long strands into two groups, A and B; Twist A tightly round the thick ends in B (see figs 3 and 4, page 62). The thick ends must be well wedged to stop the loop from coming undone under tension **(4)**. Slip a finger into the loop and pull it hard towards you to test its resistance.

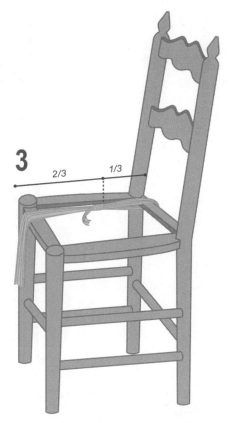

3 2/3 1/3

First strand

Continue to twist the rush regularly to create the first strand. It should be long enough to form the front left-hand corner. Pull firmly on the strand before creating the corner.

Pass the strand over crosspiece B, bring it out in the center of the seat, and pass it over crosspiece A **(5)**. Pack it as closely as possible against the chair-leg.

Pull the strand towards the second corner, keeping up the tension. Pass it over crosspiece C, bring it out in the center and pass it over crosspiece B. Pack it closely against the chair-leg **(6)**.

As soon as the second corner is formed, don't add any rush to the strand. It should be thin and long enough to pass over the back right-hand corner on crosspiece D. Keeping it tight, attach it to the lower back crosspiece with a clothes peg **(7)**. This part of the weaving is left as it is for a while. As it will be blocked during the following steps, it shouldn't be too thick.

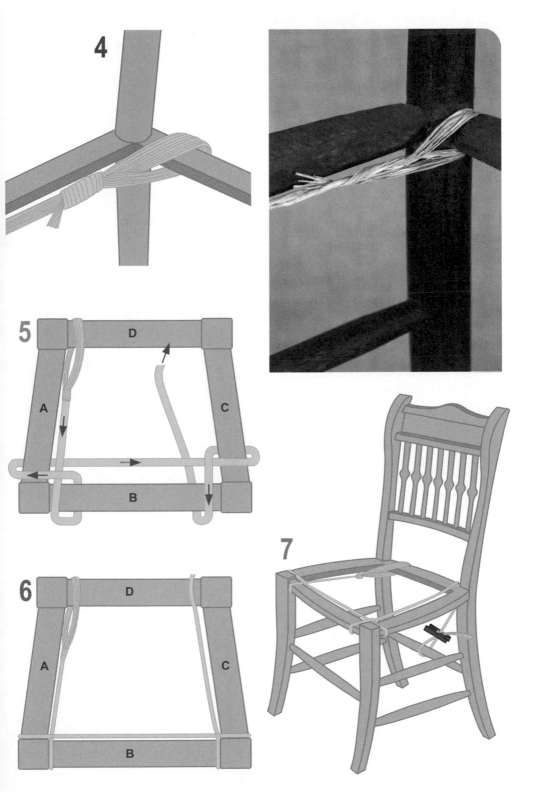

Second strand

Start the second strand by taking enough threads to form a single strand the same size as the first. Push the tuft through the starting loop made by the first strand. Twist the thick ends with the long strands as with the first loop, being careful to create your strand in the same direction as the first one. Make sure that the strand is firmly fixed to the first **(1)**.

Continue making the strand, making sure it has an even thickness. It must be able to be tightened as firmly as the first. Check to make sure that its loop is solidly fixed and won't come undone. Pass the strand over crosspiece B and the under it. Bring it out in the center and pull it towards the right-hand corner. Pass it over crosspiece C, then under it and bring it out in the center. Form the corner by passing over crosspiece B. Bring it out in the center **(2)**. As with the first, the strand should be thin but solid after the second corner.

Fix it on the lower crosspiece next to the first strand **(3)** Pack the second strand closely against the first. From the beginning of the work, keep the corners at right-angles.

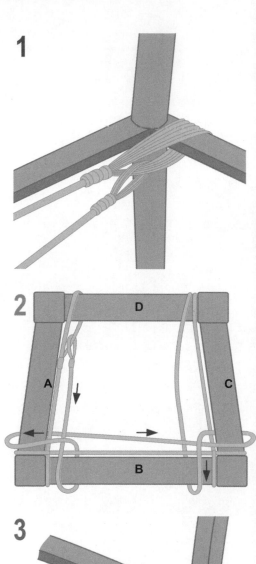

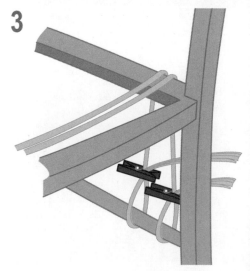

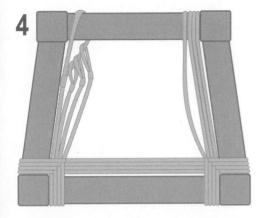

Following strands

Continue to add strands one after the other in the same way: attach them to the starting loop then once the corners are formed, fix them to the back mower bar next to each other, using clothes pegs **(4)**.

The number of strands needed will depend on the distance you need to make up between the front and back of the chair. Measure the distance regularly until the length between the weave at the front is equal to the back crosspiece **(5)** (Measure the backcross bar from leg to leg, without taking the starting loop or the waiting strands into account). Once you have re-established a square, pack the front strands closely together to double check the distance and top make sure that the corners are at correct right-angles. If necessary, correct the angles with the packing tool (see fig 5, page 66). If the starting loop breaks, replace it with cord, threaded through each loop and solidly knotted **(6)**.

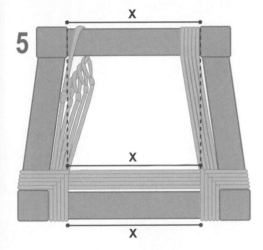

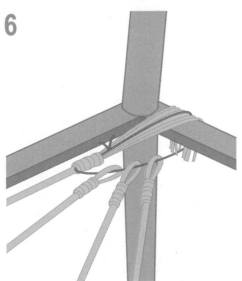

Blocking the waiting strands

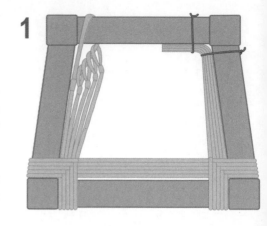

Detach the strands by removing the clothes-pegs, except for the last one. Untwist them and gather them into one tuft. Remove a few threads to thin out the tuft. Without twisting it, lay the tuft on the edge of the seat. Detach the last strand and join it to the tuft. You must keep the whole tuft and strand tight so that the front corners don't get deformed. Flatten the tuft against the right-hand crosspiece and block it with a thin but solid cord, knotted round the crosspiece at 2cm from the back corner. Fix it to the back crosspiece with another cord, making sure that it marries the interior of the angle **(1)**. Cut the blocked tuft at about 10cm from the right-hand back corner.

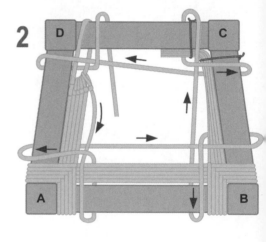

Last strand

Fix the last strand of the starting loop, as before, next to the others. Form the front corners A and B then the back corner C, keeping the strand tight so that the blocked tuft of rush in the corner flattens perfectly against the wood and doesn't deform the corner with its thickness.

Make sure that the corner forms a right-angle from the beginning of the operation. To create the back corner D, pass the strand over the starting loop by placing it close against the chair leg and pulling it very tight to stop it becoming deformed by the thick-ness of the loop **(2 & 3)**. Do the second round in the same way. You can now cut away the cords holding the tuft, as it is now blocked by the two rounds. Continuethe reseating in the same way as for a stool. Keep

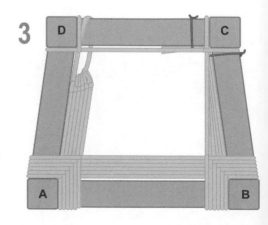

the corners at right-angles by measuring them regularly. Pack the round as you go along. Tighten the strands and pack them every third round with the packing tool.

ROUNDED CROSSPIECES

This is often the case with the side crosspieces. The outer length is therefore superior to the inner length (4). You will quickly notice while you are doing the corners. Indeed, if the strand is perfectly even and if you pack the rounds against each other, the angle will rapidly become acute (5). To get round this defect, slightly enlarge the strand in the place where the crosspiece has a larger width (6). This will avoid spaces in the weave, and the effect won't be noticeable when the chair is finished.

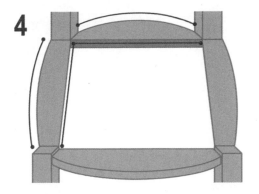

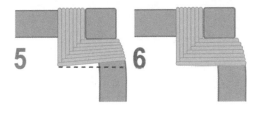

SHORTER SIDE CROSSPIECES

Once the square is re-established, the side crosspieces are shorter than those at the front and the back (7). In this case the sides will be finished before the front and the back. The measurements taken between the angles are different: the distance X is the same between corners C/D and A/B; the distance Y is the same between corners B/C and A/D (8).

Fill the front and back crosspieces using an eight-cane weave (see page 73). The reseating design ends with a small horizontal bar in the center of the seat.

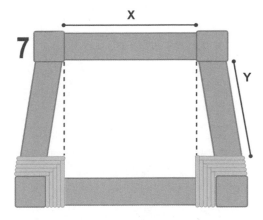

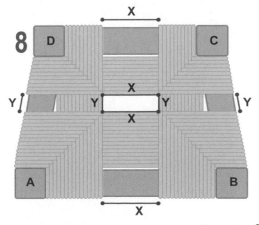

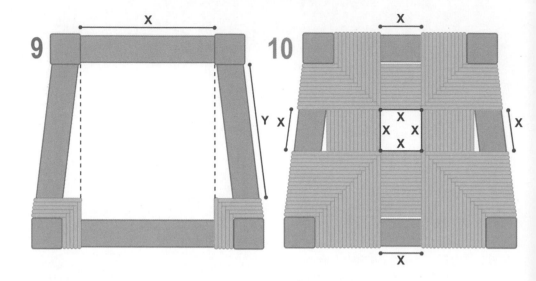

FOUR EQUAL CROSSPIECES

Once you have re-established the square, the length to fill is equal on each of the crosspieces **(9)**. In this case you will do an equal number of rounds on the sides as on the front and back crosspieces. The distance between the corners is the same **(10)**. The work will end at the point where the angle cross-lines all meet evenly at the center.

Padding and finishing

To pad the chair seat you will use the same method as padding a stool.

SHORTER SIDE CROSSPIECES

Proceed in the same way as for a rectangular stool, that is to say, by padding the sides before starting on an eight-cane weave. Pack the rounds closely against each other. Leave the rush to dry out for a few days to see if you can add another round or two on the sides and then start on the eight-cane weave (see page 73). Pad the front, then the back. Leave the rush to dry out again to see if you can add another round or two of eight-cane weave. Stop the strand definitively on the underside of the chair once you are sure that the rounds, once dried, won't retract any further.

Two-strand method

This way of "re-establishing the square" is a bit more complicated for beginners, but it has the advantage of being more discrete than the loop method. This latter method is only used when the difference between the front and back crosspieces is moderate (which is the case for ordinary chairs). Sometimes, however, the front crosspiece is almost twice as long as the back one (often found in armchairs). It is therefore impossible to attach a sufficient number of strands to the starting loop, because they would cause too large a thickness in the corners D and C, deforming the weave.

The two-strand method is therefore necessary for chairs that have a large difference in length to fill in, but it can also be used on ordinary chairs. It is recommended although it needs greater attention than the loop method.

Two strands are worked on at the same time. They form the corners A and B at each round, but only make corners C and D every other round. This means that the reseating advances faster in front. Start the first strand

on the left-hand corner of the back crosspiece by making a small loop in which only one strand is attached. Make the corners A and B, keeping the strand's thickness even. Don't thin it out after making corner B: it should have a regular thickness until the moment it is no longer needed. Attach it, keeping it stretched tightly, onto a bar at the back with a clothes pin.

Start the second strand in the starting loop. Do corners A and B. Use the same strand to make corner C. Beforehand, detach the first strand and flatten it on the inside of the angle, so that it is blocked by the second strand **(1)**. Make sure that the first strand is properly tightened. Continue with the second strand to make the corner D, blocking the first strand on the inside of the angle **(2)**. Beforehand, make sure that the first strand has kept its initial diameter and that it is properly twisted; if necessary add a few threads of rush before taking it to corner D. Make corner D by passing over the starting loops. Pack the corner so that it remains at a right-angle.

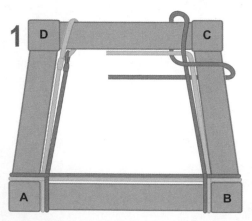

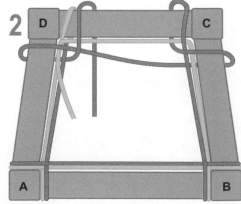

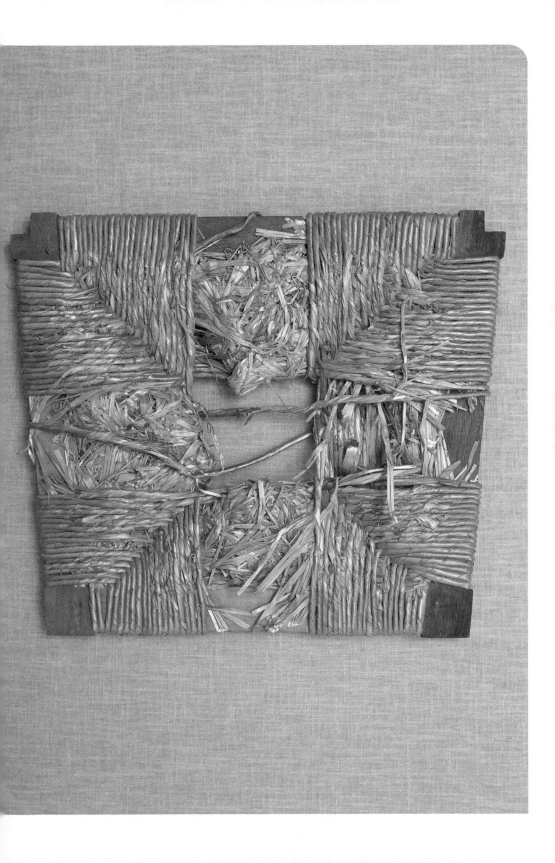

You will have two rounds at the front for one round at the back. You will be back at the starting point, where the first strand begins at corner D. You will continue with the second strand; the first is left waiting, ready to go on the next round.

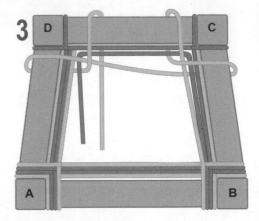

Make the corners A and B with the second strand, bring it back to corner C and then stop by fixing it with a clothes peg to the lower bar. Take up the first strand at its starting point D. Twist is and add threads long enough to form corners A and B. Stretch it tightly towards corner A, being careful not to deform corner D with the second strand. Make corners A and B. Detach the second strand and block it in the angle that form corner C with the first strand. The second strand should be flattened on the inside of the frame so that it is invisible. Make corner D with the first strand, once again blocking the second strand in the angle. Now it is the second strand that is left waiting to start the following round **(3)**. Make angles A and B with the first strand, stop it close against corner C, and restart with the second strand and so on until you have re-established the square.

To know when the square is formed, measure the lengths of wood at the front and at the back that need to be covered from time to time until they are equal **(4)**. When the square is re-established, continue to work with the current strand. Block the other strand on the inside of corner A when you make its next angle, in the same way as corners C and D. Block it on the inside of angles B, C and D without adding any extra rush. Continue the work as with a stool.

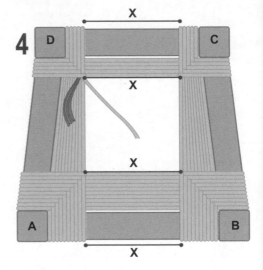

Tip

At first you might confuse the strands. To avoid mistaking them, remember that each time you stop a strand, you fix it close against corner C; each time you take up a strand it will start in corner D. By paying a little attention you will soon recognize the strand stopped on corner C and the strand waiting on corner D.

Appendices

Glossary

The words marked with an asterisk are further explained in the glossary.

General vocabulary

Apron. The fixed part that surrounds the seat*. The seat's crosspiece* form the apron.

Armrests. The lateral part of a chair, also simply called "arms."

Ceruse. A paint finish in white or pastel through which the fibers can be seen.

Coil. Circular bundle of vegetable fibers.

Crosspieces. Usually wooden elements that join the vertical parts of a chair (uprights*, legs*).

Frame. Usually made of wood, the frame can be removed. The cane* or rush* is woven onto it. It can be the seat* frame or the back* frame or can refer to part of another piece of furniture, such as the lid of a chest, a shelf or a table top.

Hank. Bundle of vegetable fibers where they are folded several times over and attached in a way so that they don't get tangled up.

Legs. The vertical elements which raise the chair, or the bottom of any piece of furniture off the floor.

Seat. The part of a chair you sit on. The depth of a standard chair seat is between 45 and 55 cm.

Soaking. Immersing vegetable fibers in water to make them supple before using them.

Sweating. Keeping the threads* in a damp cloth so that they stay supple after soaking.

Thread. Term used for rush stalks.

Uprights. The vertical elements that are part of the structure of the armrests* and the back of a chair.

Caning

Awl. Tool used to separate the weave.

Binding. Last step in caning which consists of fixing a large band of cane* around the frame* to hide the holes.

Cane. Flat rattan* rod with its bark measuring from 1.5 to 4mm wide.

Comb. This tool is used for "combing"* Traditionally made of wood or metal, modern caning combs are made of plastic and are sold in packs offering several different spacing between the teeth.

Combing. This operation tightens and straightens the weave. To be effective, combing should be done on damp cane.

Dowels. These are used to block the cane in the holes in the frame*.

Finishing. This consists of cutting the overlapping cane close to the wood under the seat. The cane can then be left as it is, or tinted, ceruse* or painted.

Flat needles. Metal needles that make laying vertical cane strands*.

Laying the diagonal cane rods. Third step in caning, which consists of weaving the cane diagonally through the vertical* and horizontal* cane. The cane* used is large, but not doubled.

Laying the horizontal cane rods. Second step in caning, which consists of weaving the cane horizontally through the vertical* cane. Two rods are used, progressing from the back of the chair towards the front.

Laying the vertical cane rods. First step in caning which consists of stretching the vertical rods across the frame* along its width. Two rounds* are carried out in opposite directions to double each rod.

Rattan. Creeper of the palm family, both creeping and climbing and which can reach several hundreds of meters long. Once stripped of its silica, its leaves and its roots, the rods are left to dry out and then used for creating different products, including spun rattan used in basket-weaving and cane* used in caning seats.

Round. Movement of a rod from one end of the frame to another.

Wire caning tool. A tool consisting of a wooden handle and a mettle wire folded in an inverted "V". Used for laying diagonal* cane, it allows you to weave the rod without having to catch it with your hand under the seat.

Rush

Band.   Synonym for rush-guard*.

Eight-cane weave.   Filling the central part of a rectangular or trapezoid seat.

Finishing.   Removing the sticking-out little "beards" of rush by cutting them close to the weave with a pair of scissors.

Marsh grass.   Grass from the Carex family that grows in damp areas. Different species are used in different regions. Marsh grass is cut under water and then dried out. It can be used as it is for a rustic effect or covered with rye straw during weaving.

Packing tool.   Wooden, metal or plastic tool that looks a bit like a paper knife, used for tightening* and repositioning the strands* after each round*.

Padding.   The operation consisting of slipping rush plugs between the upper and lower weave to tighten it and to add volume.

Raffia.   Fiber that comes from the leaves of a species of palm. Generally raffia is covered with rye straw*.

Re-establishing the square.   Weaving done on one crosspiece when it is longer than its opposite, as in trapezoid seats, to achieve a central square or rectangular area.

Rye straw.   It is harvested while still supple, before the grain matures. Traditionally left to dry out in the fields so that the sun bleaches it. Rye straw can be left as it is (blonde) or tinted.

Strand.   A cord made up of several threads* of rush. Traditionally the strand is twisted as weaving is carried out.

Straw guard.   Bands* of wood fixed around the chair seat to protect the edges of the weave.

Tamping iron.   Wooden or metal tool used for padding*.

Tightening.   This is done at different stages of the work and consists of packing the weave after leaving it to dry out and retract.

Twisted straw.   Strand* of straw ready to use, sold in coils*.

Metric conversion chart

10mm=1cm
100cm=1m

Centimeters	Inches
1cm	25/64 in.
2cm	25/32 in.
3cm	13/16 in.
4cm	1³⁷⁄₆₄ in.
5cm	1³¹⁄₃₂ in.
6cm	2²³⁄₆₄ in.
7cm	2¾ in.
8cm	3⁵⁄₃₂ in.
9cm	3³⁵⁄₆₄ in.
10cm	3¹⁵⁄₁₆ in.
11cm	4²¹⁄₆₄ in.
12cm	4²³⁄₃₂ in.
13cm	5⅛ in.
14cm	5³³⁄₆₄ in.
15cm	5²⁹⁄₃₂ in.
16cm	6¹⁹⁄₆₄ in.
17cm	6¹¹⁄₁₆ in.
18cm	7³⁄₃₂ in.
19cm	7³¹⁄₆₄ in.
20cm	7⅞ in.
21cm	8¹⁷⁄₆₄ in.
22cm	8²¹⁄₃₂ in.
23cm	9¹⁄₁₆ in.
24cm	9²⁹⁄₆₄ in.
25cm	9²⁷⁄₃₂ in.
26cm	10¹⁵⁄₆₄ in.
27cm	10⅝ in.
28cm	11¹⁄₃₂ in.
29cm	11²⁷⁄₆₄ in.
30cm	11¹³⁄₁₆ in.
31cm	12¹³⁄₆₄ in.
32cm	12¹⁹⁄₃₂ in.
33cm	12⁶³⁄₆₄ in.
34cm	13²⁵⁄₆₄ in.
35cm	13²⁵⁄₃₂ in.
36cm	14¹¹⁄₆₄ in.
37cm	14⁹⁄₁₆ in.
38cm	14⁶¹⁄₆₄ in.
39cm	15²³⁄₆₄ in.

Millimeters	Inches
1mm	3/64 in.
2mm	5/64 in.
3mm	1/8 in.
4mm	5/32 in.
5mm	13/64 in.
6mm	15/64 in.
7mm	9/32 in.
8mm	5/16 in.
9mm	23/64 in.
10mm	25/64 in.
11mm	7/16 in.
12mm	15/32 in.
13mm	33/64 in.
14mm	35/64 in.
15mm	19/32 in.
16mm	5/8 in.
17mm	43/64 in.
18mm	45/64 in.
19mm	3/4 in.
20mm	25/32 in.
21mm	53/64 in.
22mm	55/64 in.
23mm	29/32 in.
24mm	15/16 in.
25mm	63/64 in.

Meters	Feet
1m	3ft. 3⅜ in.
2m	6ft. 6⁴⁷⁄₆₄ in.
3m	9ft. 10⁷⁄₆₄ in.
4m	13ft. 1³¹⁄₆₄ in.
5m	16ft. 4²⁷⁄₃₂ in.
6m	19ft. 8⁷⁄₃₂ in.
7m	22ft. 11¹⁹⁄₃₂ in.
8m	26ft. 2⁶¹⁄₆₄ in.
9m	29ft. 6²¹⁄₆₄ in.
10m	32ft. 9⁴⁵⁄₆₄ in.
11m	36ft. 1⁵⁄₆₄ in.
12m	39ft. 4⁷⁄₁₆ in.
13m	42ft. 7¹³⁄₁₆ in.
14m	45ft. 1¹³⁄₁₆ in.
15m	49ft. 2³⁵⁄₆₄ in.

Notes

Acknowledgements
The photographer and publisher wish to thank:
M. Lopes, of the Chaisier* workshop in Paris;
Mme Toussaint, of the Les Chaises de Beynes*
workshop in Paris;
M. Neves, of the L'Artisan Rempailleur* workshop in Paris;
Rose Delaunay, of the Cannepaille* workshop in
Villaines-les-Rochers;
Évelyne Desserrières, of the Canne et Paille Tradition*
workshop in Sainte-Julie;
Michèle Raoux, of the Couleur Paille* workshop in
Brusquet;
M. and Mme Szepes, of the Le Rustique* workshop in
Châtel-Montagne;
Guillaume Dubois and Les Combustibles, "bistro culturiste",
rue Abel, Paris;
Marie Pieroni, for her investment and her many
contributions.
Thanks to Agnès Busière, my publisher,
for trusting me.

Originally printed in France by IME.
© Fleurus Éditions, 2010
Legal deposit: March 2010
ISBN: 978-2-215-10223-6

Editorship:
Christophe Savouré
Publishing:
Agnes Busiere assisted by Marion Dahyot
Art Direction:
Laurent Quellet and Julie Pauwels
Photography:
Jérôme Pallé
Illustrations:
Marie Pieroni
Production:
Anne Floutier and Thierry Dubus
Photoengraving:
Alliage

The Great Book of Cardboard Furniture: Step-by-Step Techniques and Designs. Kiki Carton. Packed with 320+ color images and patterns, here are detailed step-by-step techniques for building nine furniture designs, including chic chairs, a giraffe-shaped chest of drawers for a child's rooms, and an ultra-modern coffee table. This is an ideal home decor how-to book for anyone looking to repurpose cardboard and easily build functional and stylish furniture.

| Size: 8½" x 11" | 321 color photos & patterns | 128 pp. |
| ISBN: 978-0-7643-4151-9 | soft cover | $24.99 |

Rib Baskets. *Revised & Expanded 2nd Edition.* Jean Turner Finley. With 231 images and 107 diagrams, this revised how-to guide offers general techniques and tips for the successful weaving of 14 rib baskets. Chapters on basketry tools, materials, and the components of a rib basket are included, as are answers to frequently asked questions.

| Size: 8½" x 11" | 115 color & 116 b/w images | 107 patterns | 88 pp. |
| ISBN: 978-0-7643-4177-9 | | soft cover | $19.99 |

Old New England Splint Baskets and How to Make Them. John E. McGuire. The master basketmaker shares techniques developed over many years. Beautiful color photographs of antique New England baskets inspire readers to adapt the step-by-step instructions to create three new baskets: a round, rectangular, and square-to-round basket with traditional techniques. A unique chapter on the old tools and molds is fascinating reading to all who enjoy antique baskets.

| Size: 8½" x 11" | 100s of photos & drawings | 100 pp. |
| ISBN: 0-88740-045-0 | soft cover | $14.95 |

Do-It-Yourself Tailored Slipcovers. Sophia Sevo. A talented seamstress shares her tips and techniques for creating tailored slipcovers for a sofa bed headboard, and a variety of chair forms (wingback, bergere, club, and contemporary styles). Be inspired by detailed color images and instructions.

| Size: 8½" x 11" | 136 color photos | 112 pp. |
| ISBN: 978-0-7643-2972-2 | soft cover | $19.99 |

Upholstery, Drapes, and Slipcovers: How-to Repair and Make Them Yourself. Dorothy Wagner. Professional methods for re-covering upholstery, wonderful ideas for adding glamour to bed headboards, making custom drapes and curtains, and creating beautiful, custom-fitted slipcovers. Includes simple projects, like how to make pillows and pads, and tips on cleaning your household textiles, are included.

| Size: 6" x 9" | 251 illustrations and 31 b/w photos | Index | 248 pp. |
| ISBN: 978-0-7643-2745-2 | softcover | | $19.95 |

Schiffer Publishing, Ltd. 4880 Lower Valley Rd., Atglen, PA 19310 Phone (610) 593-1777 Fax (610) 593-2002 E-mail: Info@schifferbooks.com